AF812600

# Financing Health and Social Care

"Without doubt, the most important update and reminder of economic reasoning and evidence as to why our publicly-funded health care systems need protection and expansion, even into areas such as social care. Professor Donaldson's work over four decades has had a tremendous impact on decision makers, economic advisors, fellow researchers and learners and I anticipate this book will be no exception."

—Craig Mitton, *Professor in School of Population and Public Health, University of British Columbia*

"Leading world expert, and I don't say that lightly. Everyone should read the chapter on economics of pandemics."

—Bruce Hollingsworth, *Professor of Health Economics, Lancaster University*

"I thoroughly enjoyed reading this wonderful book. At a time when many health systems are in flux, it provides a reminder of the kinds of health system arrangements that provide for equity and efficiency. It contains lessons not only for UK policy, but also for those concerned with developing, implementing and sustaining Universal Health Coverage. It should be read by health economists, health ministers and their advisors across the globe."

—Susan Cleary, *Professor of Health Economics, University of Cape Town, South Africa*

Cam Donaldson

# Financing Health and Social Care

## Bringing Health Economics Back into Public Policy

palgrave
macmillan

Cam Donaldson
Glasgow Caledonian University
Glasgow, UK

ISBN 978-3-031-86768-2 ISBN 978-3-031-86769-9 (eBook)
https://doi.org/10.1007/978-3-031-86769-9

© The Author(s), under exclusive license to Springer Nature Switzerland AG 2025

This work is subject to copyright. All rights are solely and exclusively licensed by the Publisher, whether the whole or part of the material is concerned, specifically the rights of translation, reprinting, reuse of illustrations, recitation, broadcasting, reproduction on microfilms or in any other physical way, and transmission or information storage and retrieval, electronic adaptation, computer software, or by similar or dissimilar methodology now known or hereafter developed.
The use of general descriptive names, registered names, trademarks, service marks, etc. in this publication does not imply, even in the absence of a specific statement, that such names are exempt from the relevant protective laws and regulations and therefore free for general use.
The publisher, the authors and the editors are safe to assume that the advice and information in this book are believed to be true and accurate at the date of publication. Neither the publisher nor the authors or the editors give a warranty, expressed or implied, with respect to the material contained herein or for any errors or omissions that may have been made. The publisher remains neutral with regard to jurisdictional claims in published maps and institutional affiliations.

Cover illustration: © Melisa Hasan

This Palgrave Macmillan imprint is published by the registered company Springer Nature Switzerland AG
The registered company address is: Gewerbestrasse 11, 6330 Cham, Switzerland

If disposing of this product, please recycle the paper.

*Diane, no other words suffice*

*Acknowledgements* There are many people to whom I am eternally grateful for giving me the confidence, encouragement and ability to write this book.

I was given a good start in health economics, by mentors such as Alan Maynard (York), John Forbes (Glasgow, now Limerick), Ian Russell and John Bond (Newcastle) and Gavin Mooney (Aberdeen). Senga Bond, also of Newcastle, has always believed in me and given me the confidence to do stuff differently. In my early days at York, I shared an office with Steve Birch. Now located in Queensland, Steve has been great friend and critic over the past 40 years.

As many of my colleagues know, I love working in teams! Through that, I have worked with many great people over the years, and the ones who will recognise some of the material in the book are Rachel Baker, Angela Bate, Olga Biosca, Stirling Bryan, Gillian Currie, Karen Gerard, Steve Jan, Emily Lancsar, Paul Leak, Helen Mason, Braden Manns, Neil McHugh, Craig Mitton, Gillian Murray, Alastair Noble, Stuart Peacock, Jim Rankin, Angela Robinson, Michael Roy, Danny Ruta, Mandy Ryan, Phil Shackley, Alan Shiell and Virginia Wiseman.

Some of the material in Chapter 3 was written with my friend and colleague, Dr Danny Ruta and, also in Chapter 3, my thanks go to Cathie Russell, Nick Kempe and Jim Pearson for their insights on social care and care home funding. The general practitioner behind the wise words expounded near the end of Chapter 4 is Dr Alastair Noble. But much of the material in that chapter has been developed over a 25-year period with Professor Craig Mitton of the University of British Columbia.

I am deeply indebted to friends and colleagues who read drafts, pointed me in the direction of important literature and ideas to include and who gave me time to write. Thanks to Rachel Baker, David Bryant, Diane Donaldson, Linda Fenocchi, Helen Jones, Paul Leak, Helen Mason, Craig Mitton and James Stuart.

Finally, I also cannot thank my family enough for the love and support they have given me over the years, permitting me to accumulate the experience to allow me to write this piece. Love you guys, always.

*Competing Interests* The author has no competing interests to declare that are relevant to the content of this manuscript.

# Contents

# About the Author

**Cam Donaldson** is Emeritus Yunus Chair at Glasgow Caledonian University (GCU) and Professor of Health Economics at the Australian National University. From 2010–24, he held the Yunus Chair at GCU and, from 2016–21, served as Pro Vice Chancellor Research there. Previously, Cam held the Health Foundation Chair in Health Economics at Newcastle University and the Svare Chair in Health Economics at the University of Calgary. He first become a professor of health economics in 1996 whilst at the Health Economics Research Unit at the University of Aberdeen.

Cam has received numerous competitive awards in recognition of his research, having been:

- an inaugural National Institute for Health Research Senior Investigator;
- a Public Services Fellow in the Advanced Institute for Management Research, funded by the UK's Economic and Social Research Council;
- a Canadian Institutes for Health Research Senior Investigator; and
- a Senior Scholar, funded by the Alberta Heritage Foundation for Medical Research.

Cam has published over 300 peer-reviewed articles in economics, medical, health policy and health management journals and (co-)authored or edited several books on health economics and public service delivery. In

2025, Cam was listed by Research.com in the top 300 Economics and Finance Scientists globally (28 in the UK) all-time by citation and publications. In 2023, he was listed in Stanford University's list of the world's top 2% of scientists, and, in 2022, was elected to the Fellowship of the Royal Society of Edinburgh.

Cam lives near Stonehaven, in Aberdeenshire, with his wife Diane.

# List of Figures

# List of Tables

CHAPTER 1

# Whatever Happened to Health Economics?

**Abstract** There are tried and trusted ways to fund and provide health care according to both economic theory and evidence. Yet health economics seems to have lost its wider influence and several policy distractions abound, diverting politicians from the key global messages. Most countries are heading towards Universal Health Coverage in one form or other, with some form of collective insurance at its heart. The case for this, from an economic perspective, needs to be reiterated. But a publicly financed health and social care system does not avoid the issue of claims continually outstripping resource availability. Thus, we also need economics to assist with big questions such as the role of the private sector, use of frameworks for setting priorities, workforce planning and pay, and preparation for future pandemics. Throughout, we will refer to the thoughts of the originator of the UK's National Health Service, Aneurin Bevan. Although he had much to say of relevance, he neither fully articulated the economic case for an NHS nor how to use economics in its design and management. This volume also seeks to fill those gaps.

**Keywords** Health and social care · NHS · Universal Health Coverage · Economics

© The Author(s), under exclusive license to Springer Nature Switzerland AG 2025

C. Donaldson, *Financing Health and Social Care*,
https://doi.org/10.1007/978-3-031-86769-9_1

The world is full of complexities, for which expert advice is required. Health is no exception. We visit our (medical) doctor for advice on what to do about the minor and major ailments that afflict us. Not all doctors are perfect, but, for the most part, their expertise also cuts out the 'quackery'; eliminating the useless remedies and even placebos that we might often be tempted to try. The same is true of advice about health care financing and provision. From an economic perspective, health care is one of the most complex 'goods'. As a society, we want answers to recurring questions of how best to fund and provide it. As a qualified (PhD) doctor, and based on over 40 years of practice, I hope that I can impart my advice with respect to these, and other, questions that ordinary members of the public (much like patients) want answers to. My expertise lies in health economics, which, despite some influence in the assessment of health technologies, has appeared little in recent years with respect to debates on these wider and system-level issues. Note that the role of economics was particularly absent in policy discussions with respect to the recent Covid-19 pandemic.

The reason this is harmful to society is that, perhaps without realising it, those in power, especially if reluctant to think about asking the public to pay increased taxes, often resort to false remedies and placebos. These are policy 'solutions', which despite appearing and often being dressed up to do so, offer no real benefit. Continuing the medical analogy, these placebos provide short-term reassurance that something is being done, but without getting at the fundamentals of the condition. Contradictions and double-speak abound. Politicians consistently proclaim that health care should be universally available and free at the point of delivery. This also fits with the global initiative, promoted by the World Health Organisation, to move all countries towards Universal Health Coverage (UHC). Such statements are well-intentioned. But they leave open major questions which are the subject matter of this book. What will be the funding basis of the system—public, private or mixed? Might there be a role for the private sector in provision of services, even if publicly funded? How might we sustain and develop the oft-neglected and accompanying social care system? Even if there are solutions to such questions, this will not allow us to avoid questions as to how we deal with competing claims on limited resources and how to staff and best incentivise the health workforce. In addressing these questions in subsequent chapters, we will lay out common questions and proposed solutions as well as addressing equally common, but false, remedies proposed, and sometimes enacted.

For example, in Chapter 2 we will tackle the question of how to achieve the goal of free health care for all. If readers will indulge me in thinking of health care as a 'commodity', it will be shown that, due to the comprehensiveness of market failure for such a commodity, publicly funded health care systems are not only more equitable but also more efficient than leaving financing to the market. Why, then, do we consistently hear about alternatives which at best offer 'sticking plaster' solutions—these being user charges, switching from one basic system to another (e.g. from NHS to social insurance, or vice versa), hypothecated taxes for the NHS and social care or using supplemental (private) insurance to relieve pressure on the public system—without addressing the fundamental issues of resourcing the system?

Having dealt with the financing of the system, we then move, in Chapter 3, to demand-side socialism. Despite market failure leading to a case for public financing on the demand side of health care markets, might there still be a role for the private sector in provision? To address this question, we need to separate out the financing of health care from its provision. Then, the possibilities for a role for the private sector can be demonstrated. It will be shown that proposals to ban private provision ignore evidence and also the historical foundations of the NHS.

It is also time, in my view, to extend the notion of demand-side socialism to social care. Of course, social care covers a myriad of personal and practical support services to enable those requiring additional assistance to maintain their independence and quality of life. For the purposes of the book, however, this will be limited to those areas more related to health; those providing health-related care at home and in care homes for vulnerable groups, mostly older people who are physically or mentally infirm. The complexities of social care are, in part, what makes its reform, in the form of a National Care Service (NCS) so challenging, especially when parts of it—the parts focused on in this book—might be better integrated with the health care system. Nevertheless, it is now recognised that there is no point fixing health care without fixing social care, as the two act in parallel. A well-functioning social care system helps prevent people entering the health care system and also facilitates their earlier discharge. Therefore, in Chapters 2 and 3, consideration is also given to how the market failure arguments apply to social care. We review the funding system in the United Kingdom (UK)—although its complexity can be transferred to other countries—and make the case for a system of financing similar to that for health care. There, it is important to challenge the notion that reform of the financing of social care (in the UK) is unaffordable. We show that it would cost very little. Indeed, given the growing number of people with dementia in the social care system, there is an inevitability to the case made, as there is no reason why the market failure arguments applied to funding services for people with other medical conditions, most of whom just happen to use the NHS, should not also apply to this group, who just happen to reside in social care.

The *quid pro quo* for all of the above is addressed in Chapter 4. How do we set priorities in health and social care? A common way of thinking, here, is that public funding somehow eliminates the need to manage scarcity. Claims on such systems, like the NHS, will always outstrip the resources we have available to put into them. Here, we outline the main principles behind an economic approach to managing such scarcity, along with some short case studies of using these in practice. Another placebo to be dealt with here is the perception that having national-level health technology assessment (HTA) agencies addresses the issue of scarcity. How do we know HTA agencies have made our health care systems more efficient? Should we try to make the practice of priority setting more widespread, even going as far as localities? We need to move away from management frameworks that take on the appearance of solving issues of resource scarcity, but without facing up to the real choices that have to be made. In seeking to move health care managers away from succumbing to fads and gimmicks, we need to make the health economics frameworks work for them. We will conclude Chapter 4 by offering such a framework.

With staff being the largest and key resource in health and social care, it is essential, in Chapter 5, to address two aspects of the workforce. The first is on how we should pay professions and, of course, how much. From research, there are tried and tested lessons that essentially lead us to a system of remuneration, especially for doctors as the main controllers of resource use in the system, that is based on 'horses for courses'; that is, the system of remuneration will be mixed, across salaries, fees-for-items-of-service, capitation and others, and based, in any particular context, on what funders (usually governments) are trying to achieve. False remedies, here, come from all sides of the remuneration debate, including health economists, who might argue that one specific form of payment is wrong. Secondly, we need to decide on how many of each category of staff we need. How do we plan for that? There are straightforward ways of doing this that have only rarely been implemented. It should be clear by now that, on workforce planning, the previously proposed remedies have obviously not worked. Yet, we keep returning to the same well, reinforcing vested interests, and arriving at periodic staffing crises, of which the current one—post-Covid-pandemic, post-Brexit and post-inflationary spike—is one of the worst and seemingly (but only seemingly) intractable.

It would seem remiss not to reflect on the role of economics during the recent Covid-19 pandemic, and we turn to this in Chapter 6. It went wrong for health economics, given its lack of visibility at a time when the management of scarcity—the lifeblood of economics—was key. The management of resources during the pandemic was also a disaster for some countries and parts of the world, and the UK was no exception. Taking a look back at the pandemic experience provides many lessons for moving forward. This is especially important as much misdirection lies in governments consistently blaming current crises on the past pandemic, when the key factor was lack of preparation; that is, the system was broken before the pandemic, and due to policy choices of successive governments, was already running at close to its maximum capacity. To avoid such mistakes repeating themselves, are there particular systems and ways of organising such systems that worked better than others in achieving the ultimate outcome—minimising deaths? What could economics have done to inform management of resources in the midst of the pandemic (allocations of resources to testing, ventilation and temporary hospital sites) and, more widely, considerations of 'health versus the economy'? How can economic notions of market failure and the value of life be used to best effect in aiding policy-making amidst such moments of crisis? Similar to lessons from Chapter 4, recognising and manging the requisite trade-offs will minimise the need to make them. Managing health and the economy together in one framework can work to the betterment of both.

Readers will be wondering what all these proposals will cost the general public. Therefore, we will, in Chapter 7, as well as summarising the general messages to be taken from the book, address the issue of the price of the prescription. Astonishingly, it will be seen that such costs are not great and that much of the work has been done for us by expert commissions that the politicians seem to ignore. A key message that emanates from such commissions is that, despite the cost, the alternatives will be even more expensive and unfair. For the UK, that means not whether we can afford the NHS but rather can we afford not to have an NHS. The same applies to most other countries, from which some examples will be drawn as we progress through the book.

Finally, a note on where the book sits in the spectrum of policy and politics. A naive observer might be forgiven for thinking that the journey from the post-war consensus to post-pandemic demonstrates that the case for a publicly funded NHS is settled, and could even be extended to social care. The Welfare State, and within that the NHS, was one of the main pillars of the post-war concensus [1] As well as the NHS coming into being in 1948 due, in large part, to the drive of then Minister of Health Aneurin Bevan, this consensus applied to many other countries, two of which will be referred to throughout the book. Tommy Douglas, a Scotsman, was the force behind the creation of Medicare in Canada—and, in contrast to British preferences for a war hero, was also voted the Greatest Canadian [2]. Health economists, John Deeble and Richard Scotton, were two of the architects of Australia's Medicare system. Jumping forward to the present day, state intervention was crucial in getting us through the pandemic. However, this would ignore challenges to the post-war consensus expressed at the time [3] and which culminated, in the UK, in the election of Prime Minister Margaret Thatcher. How can we forget the reaction of one Tory MP to the opening ceremony of the London Olympics in 2012, in which the NHS featured strongly as a supposed demonstration of UK culture, labelling it at as 'leftie multicultural crap'? More seriously, and currently, politicians of the Left, in the UK and elsewhere, are reluctant to raise the taxes that might be required to sustain publicly funded systems providing universal coverage. Thus, to some extent, we are all Thatcher's children now.

These are political and policy tensions that underlie the book. From a Centre-Left perspective, my hope is that the resurrection of health economics in this context can help in resolving them.

## References

1. Addison P. The Road to 1945: British Politics and the Second World War. Jonathan Cape, London, 1975.
2. Stewart W. The Life and Political Times of Tommy Douglas. McArthur and Company, Toronto, 2003.
3. Jeffreys K. The Churchill Coalition and Wartime Politics, 1940–45. Manchester University Press, 1995.

CHAPTER 2

# In Place of Fear 2.0: The Efficiency and Fairness of Free Health Care for All

**Abstract** In this chapter, the comprehensive market failure of health care as a commodity is outlined. This provides the basis for why publicly funded health care is not only more equitable but also more efficient. This, more than any humanitarian basis, is why we, in the UK, have an NHS and other countries have their own systems, also dominated by government funding. Otherwise we, in the UK, would have a National Food Service as well as an NHS. The similarities between advanced economies' publicly funded health care systems, in the form of some sort of collective insurance, are more striking than any differences, many of the latter being merely artefacts of history. Such artefacts lead to policy distractions which need to be discussed and dismissed, such as user charges; switching from one basic system to another (e.g. from NHS to social insurance); a hypothecated tax for the NHS and social care; and seeking new forms of financial support, such as social impact bonds.

**Keywords** Market failure · Moral hazard · Externalities · Social insurance · Hypothecation · User charges

*Instead of writing a foreword for the book, I thought I would try to do so for each of the main chapters. When writing this book, I suggested to the publisher that we call it 'In Place of Fear, 2.0'. The reasons for this were to*

© The Author(s), under exclusive license to Springer Nature Switzerland AG 2025

C. Donaldson, *Financing Health and Social Care*,
https://doi.org/10.1007/978-3-031-86769-9_2

*pay homage to one of my heroes, Aneurin Bevan, the driving force behind the creation of the UK's NHS. When reflecting on the creation of the NHS in 'In Place of Fear' in 1952, Bevan articulated how an NHS would replace our fears not only of ill-health but also the financial ruin that could result* [1]. *However, beyond that, he never fully explored the economics of his case. All that came later,* via *other authors, and is summarised in this chapter; hence the 2.0. There are other reasons to write this piece now. The government, of which Bevan was a part, managed to put in place a universal health care system at a time when the UK was on its knees economically. That has strong parallels to today. Also, there are other, heterodox, economics-based approaches which I admire and could be used to make the case; but I also love taking standard neo-classical and welfare economics and standing them on their heads. My publisher was correct in refusing my request. She said that not many people would understand the title, and so it would not help with searching and, therefore, sales! So, I thought I would sneak it into the title of an early chapter! Also, despite what I have said, Bevan did offer many insights that can be supported by the now-developed economic case for a National Health Service. So, in most chapters, and especially this one, you will be hearing from him.*

In this chapter, the comprehensive market failure of health care as a commodity is outlined. This provides the basis for why publicly funded health care is not only more equitable but also more efficient. Given recent trends in integration of social care along with health care, it is also important to examine whether such arguments extend to government intervention with respect to funding the former; especially as, currently, in many countries, social care is the subject of more mixed (private as well as public) sources of funding than is health care.

This would seem to be in line with politicians the world over who claim that health care should be universally available and free at the point of delivery. This was certainly the case in the 2024 General Election campaign in the UK. In Scotland, too, Neil Gray, Cabinet Secretary for NHS Recovery, Health and Social Care , stated in June 2024 that he is 'open to ideas' about NHS reform whilst vowing that the service would, nevertheless, remain free at point of delivery. There is now, of course, a well-recognised global initiative to move all countries towards UHC. Such statements and initiatives do, however, leave open questions as to the funding basis for the system and whether, if continuing to fund it via taxation, there is any role for other funding sources that proponents might describe as supplemental to the basic system; these being user charges and private insurance, often promoted as helping to relieve pressure on the NHS and, hence the taxpayer. Hypothecated taxes and social insurance, too, are frequently touted as alternatives to general taxation and could still involve care being free at the point of delivery. Such supplements and alternatives, however, form the basis of placebos and political double-speak in the financing of health care, and are therefore, reviewed towards the end of this chapter.

Before getting to that, from the outset of the book, it is important to unpack what is seen by most health economists as a settled case; that a publicly financed health care system is not only more equitable but also more efficient. This is a lesson that has been learned in almost all advanced economies of the world. The elements underlying the economic notion of 'market failure', from which the case stems, were first brought together by the great Canadian economist, Robert Evans [2], reinforced by others over the years [3–5]. In economics, market failure does not equate to a dislike of free markets. Many people dislike the fact that only some people can afford luxury cars, but rarely do we hear a case being made for a National Car Service. Market failure is quite specific, arising when markets struggle to account fully for important characteristics of commodities; rendering their allocation sub-optimal relative to when governments intervene. An NHS is an extreme, but justifiable and popular, form of this, and the case will be made, here and in Chapter 3, to extend this to an NCS of some form.

Before proceeding further with describing market failure in more detail, there is obviously a valid (equity-based) humanitarian case for a free NHS. However, it is interesting that this case does not necessarily stretch to other commodities, such as food, for which, it could be argued, access is even more of a fundamental human right than access to health care. Yet we do not have a National Food Service. Apart from income supplementation on the demand side and regulation of standards on the supply side, this fundamental commodity can be provided adequately largely through market forces. So, are their additional things about the nature of health care as a 'commodity' that makes it different? Furthermore, given recent trends towards greater integration, and that human rights-based arguments have been made for greater government involvement in social care funding [6], do the market failure arguments also support such proposals?

## Market Failure and the Nature of the Commodity, Health Care

As Table 2.1 demonstrates, in most advanced economies, public funding of health care dominates and, in most countries, has increased over the 1990–2022 time period. Even where it is has decreased, the percentage of spend covered by the public purse has remained very high, the two largest drops being in countries (Czech Republic and Poland) which, in 1990, were emerging from the Soviet era. In Table 2.1, this is portrayed for countries reporting to the Organisation for Economic Cooperation and Development (OECD), showing also that this phenomenon is sustained over time. Some of the recent dominance of public sources of funding lies with the Covid-19 pandemic. But, more generally, the explanation stems from three sources of market failure discussed below.

### *The Failure of Insurance*

Without government intervention, an insurance market would develop to deal with unpredictable health care needs. However, with financial risks mitigated by insurance, costs may receive less emphasis in the decisions of consumers and providers. Indeed, this 'moral hazard' is at the root of the continuing challenge of cost inflation in US health care, exacerbated by administrative costs (of billing and advertising) which further inflate premiums; pricing people out of the market who otherwise would have insured. Several academic papers, notably those of Steffie Woolhandler and David Himmelstein [7, 8] have shown that around 30% of US health expenditure is spent on administration, twice that of the public system in Canada. It costs a lot to administer the market.

Of course, another potential moral hazard is that the act of becoming insured makes people less likely to look after themselves through health-promoting behaviours. There is little evidence for this. Such behaviours would ultimately make their way through to increased premiums and are more likely influenced by wider social determinants, such as income levels, environmental and cultural factors.

These problems exist in public systems too. But government funding and supply-side controls (limiting human and capital resource) make it easier to keep a lid on costs, despite tensions in controlling some parts of the budget (e.g. pharmaceutical costs). As regards looking after oneself, the points about wider determinants equally apply. Also, it could just as

**Table 2.1** Total health expenditure per head and per cent of total that is public, OECD countries (1990, 2022)

| *Country* | *1990 total health exp US$PPP* | *% public* | *2022 total health exp US$PPP* | *% public (2021)* | *Absolute change in % public* |
|---|---|---|---|---|---|
| Australia | 1318 | 67 | 6372 | 74 | +7 |
| Austria | 1205 | 74 | 7275 | 78 | +4 |
| Canada | 1678 | 75 | 6319 | 72 | −3 |
| Czech Rep | 576 | 96 | 4512 | 87 | −9 |
| Denmark | 1453 | 83 | 6280 | 85 | +2 |
| Finland | 1292 | 81 | 5599 | 82 | +1 |
| France | 1520 | 78 | 6630 | 79 | +1 |
| Germany | 1602 | 76 | 8011 | 79 | +3 |
| Greece | 707 | 63 | 3015 | 62 | −1 |
| Iceland | 1376 | 87 | 5314 | 84 | −3 |
| Ireland | 796 | 72 | 6047 | 78 | +6 |
| Italy | 1321 | 78 | 4291 | 75 | −3 |
| Japan | 1082 | 78 | 5251 | 85 | +7 |
| (South) Korea | 371 | 37 | 4570 | 61 | +24 |
| Luxembourg | 1486 | 93 | 6436 | 86 | −7 |
| Mexico | 260 | 41 | 1181 | 50 | +9 |
| Netherlands | 1403 | 78 | 6729 | 66 | −12 |
| N Zealand | 937 | 82 | 6061 | 79 | −3 |
| Norway | 1363 | 83 | 7771 | 86 | +3 |
| Poland | 258 | 96 | 2973 | 72 | −24 |
| Portugal | 614 | 65 | 4162 | 63 | −2 |
| Spain | 815 | 79 | 4432 | 72 | −7 |
| Sweden | 1492 | 90 | 6438 | 86 | −4 |
| Switzerland | 1782 | 68 | 8049 | 37 | v31 |
| Turkey | 171 | 61 | 1827 | 79 | +18 |
| UK | 968 | 84 | 5493 | 84 | 0 |
| USA | 2738 | 40 | 12,555 | 56 | +16 |

*Note on USA* Due to the Affordable Care Act (Obamacare) being enacted in 2014, there was a shift in the USA from voluntary to compulsory pre-payments, and, relatedly, the numbers of people with no coverage fell dramatically. Although, compulsory pre-payment may still involve private payments (e.g. user charges) being imposed later, this is by way of saying that, although the numbers in Table 2.1 do not reveal it, the situation in the USA in 2022 is markedly improved compared with 1990, with 91% population coverage. In European terms, the USA is now most similar to Switzerland and the Netherlands which also have considerable compulsory pre-payment, ensuring high rates of population coverage (100% in Netherlands and Switzerland). However, it is also important to note that compulsory private pre-payments do not achieve transfers from rich to poor or healthy to unhealthy in the ways that more public forms of financing do

*Source* OECD, Health at a Glance 2023 (https://www.oecd-ilibrary.org/social-issues-migration-health/health-at-a-glance-2023_13bdff54-en). Public funding is calculated using spending by government schemes and social health insurance

*$PPP* (Purchasing Power Parity) is a form of currency conversion making spends across countries more easily comparable

well be argued that attitudes to public systems, driven by the Common Good, render people reluctant to use them in ways that would be seen as frivolous. In any event, in either system, privately or publicly funded, introduction of financial instruments to curtail moral hazard, such as user charges, have proven to be both ineffectual and inequitable—see subsection on 'Why not user charges?' below.

For social care, similar arguments can be propounded. Social care is more difficult to characterise in the way we have done for health care as in Table 2.1, and especially across countries. In 2018, in the UK, approximately £100 billion worth of care support was provided informally (i.e. privately), with an additional £22 billion from local authorities and £11 billion funded privately [9]. A substantial, unspecified, proportion of the £22 billion comes from (private) user contributions. The question arises as to whether the three sources of market failure also apply to this more-mixed economy for social care, which may, then, justify greater amounts of public funding.

It might seem strange that social care insurance markets do not already exist. Similar to health care, there is much uncertainty as to whether such care will be needed later in life. However, it is likely the case that many people think that many of their care costs will be covered by the state and that, if required, they can call on their (largely housing) assets, if they are lucky enough to have them, to pay for accommodation. The details of financial arrangements, and their associated injustices are addressed in Chapter 3. But, already, it can be seen that there are important gaps in consumer knowledge when leaving health and social care to the vagaries of the market. This lack of knowledge is an associated aspect of market failure which we can now look at.

### *Lack of Consumer Knowledge*

Markets work well when consumers are well informed, which is not the case in health care. In health care, consumers are protected in terms of quality through (rightly) granting licence to practice to professionals with the qualifications to do so. But this inadvertently grants market power to professions, especially physicians, which requires what Evans has referred to as 'countervailing power' of government; to negotiate with professions over pay and levels of provision [10].

Such an argument is also relevant to social care, whereby providers can use their knowledge advantage to specify care packages which may not be in line with what a fully informed consumer would wish; thus, requiring government, again with its countervailing collective power, to step in.

### *Markets Don't Care; But People Do*

Insurance also excludes the less-well-off and neediest. If we think about it, a well-functioning insurance market will tailor lower premiums to those at low risk and higher premiums to those at higher risk. In health, those at higher risk tend to be less-well-off, and unable to afford cover. This is termed 'adverse selection' in the sense that those in most need end up facing the highest, and often prohibitive, premiums.

Bevan recognised this in *In Place of Fear* [1]. Reflecting on the situation in the UK pre-World War Two he states:

> We had experience of this in Britain where certain of the Approved Societies under the old National Health Insurance recruited a disproportionate number of members from industries with a high degree of sickness and accident rate and affected by serious industrial depression. The result was that these Approved Societies were compelled to curtail benefits to their members, while other societies with a different industrial composition were able to distribute the full benefits. The situation consequently helped the strong and hurt the weak. (p. 103)

Inequalities are further exacerbated in that, with the wealthier now selected into their own part of the market, higher-quality, hotel-like services can be tailored towards them due to their willingness and ability to pay. Although, as indicated above, these outcomes may be thought merely to be the product of a well-functioning market, these types of 'adverse selection' count as market failure because people care enough about them to be willing to transfer resources from the rich and more healthy to the poor and less healthy; something which markets, with their focus on individuals acting on their own behalf, fail to do and which charitable and philanthropic endeavours cannot come close to making up for. Without knowing he was articulating the economic notion of the caring externality, Bevan stated, in *In Place of Fear* [1]:

> Society becomes more wholesome, more serene, and spiritually healthier, if it knows that its citizens have at the back of their consciousness the knowledge that not only themselves, but all their fellows, have access, when ill, to the best that medical skill can provide. But private charity and endowment,

> although inescapably essential at one time, cannot meet the cost of all of this. If the job is to be done, the state must accept financial responsibility. (p. 100)

This 'caring externality' is why governments intervene in food markets too. But failures there are not comprehensive enough to warrant going further; in short, food needs are more predictable and, generally, consumers know what they like. It could also be argued that societies could deal with caring through public 'safety nets', such as Medicare and the Medicaid systems for vulnerable groups in the US. However, at least pre-Obamacare, this still left around one in six people in the US inadequately insured with multiple tiers of access to health care of variable quality. Back in 1952, Bevan had something very similar to say on this [1]:

> Some American friends tried hard to persuade me that the way out of the alleged dilemma of providing free health treatment for people able to afford to pay for it would be to fix an income limit below which treatment would be free while those above it must pay……The really objectionable feature is the creation of a two-standard health service, one below and one above the salt. It is merely the British Poor Law system over again. (p. 101)

Even with Obamacare, what the US has still not learned is that taxation is the most effective way to achieve the transfers necessary to ensure 100% coverage of its population for health care and keep administration costs down. Despite the (apparent) startling change in the percentage of health care which is public, much of this is still achieved through private insurance schemes; hopefully reflecting that the US is still on a journey towards the greater fairness and efficiency achieved in many other advanced economies. These notions of achieving financial safety for some of the population, whilst others pay more out of their own pocket (whether in direct user charges or private insurance premiums), can be reflected in social care, too, and, using the example of the UK, is delineated in more detail in Chapter 3. However, the key lesson, here and there, is that the most effective way to achieve the transfers necessary to ensure universal coverage, whether for health or social care, is through taxation. Indeed, given the positive association between wealth and health, taxation achieves the 'double whammy' of enabling transfers from the rich-and-healthy to the poor-and-less-healthy.

### *It's the Comprehensiveness of Market Failure!*

A short, but key, point to emphasise at this juncture is that, although many readers will recognise aspects of market failure in other goods, there is no good for which market failure is as comprehensive as in health care.

Our final reference to Bevan in this chapter shows his appreciation of this [1]:

> A free Health Service is a triumphant example of the superiority of collective action and public initiative applied to a segment of society where commercial principles are seen at their worst. (p. 109)

It is all of these aspects of market failure occurring together that make extensive government intervention in health care, in the case of the UK in the form of an NHS, not only more equitable but also more efficient. We have briefly indicated, and will do so in more detail in Chapters 3 and 4, that these arguments can also be extended to something like an NCS. The term 'something like' is used because, as indicated in Chapter 1, an alternative is for an NHS and aspects of social care to be integrated with each other, as already happens in many jurisdictions internationally. Before getting there though, there are several related reforms that are often put forward as 'solutions' to which we now turn in brief.

## Can We Help the NHS with Supplemental or Alternative Sources of Funds?

### *Why Not User Charges?*

A naïve observer would say that user charges could help control costs or reduce frivolous demands on the NHS. However, evidence of frivolous use by patients is hard to come by. What the evidence does show is that charges reduce demand only amongst the poor (and less healthy), have been shown not to discriminate between needed and unneeded care and do not control total costs anyway (as the system simply switches its care-giving powers to those willing and able to pay or those put-off by charges present with more-costly ailments later). This then creates a system with widening inequalities in quantity and quality of provision, much as we see when a large proportion of funding of the care system is based on such charges. Only recently, and in a universal health care system, such as

Australia, charges for Medicare out-of-hospital services and for prescription medicines have been shown to be regressive in the sense of taking up a higher proportions of disposable income amongst poorer groups [11]. Exemptions are possible, but, then, add administrative costs (of billing and collection of funds) whilst counteracting the original arguments for charges in the first place; as the exempt can access care as before whilst the non-exempt can likely afford to as well. In short, user charges are either futile, unjust or both.

### *Why Not Supplemental Health Insurance?*

Supplementary health insurance is often promoted as having the ability to relieve pressure on the NHS. Again, there is very little evidence to back this up. Most of the evidence shows the impact to be detrimental with respect to waiting lists in the public part of the system. The reasons for this are quite obvious. At any one point in time, there are only so many doctors available to provide treatment. If their attention is diverted to the private part of the system this has to be at the expense of the public part. Likely, too, patients left in the public part of the system will be in greater need of care.

Indeed, it could be argued that the most likely policy direction of government with respect to health care financing is along these lines, and that we may be at a tipping point in this regard. In 2024, the Joseph Rowntree Foundation reported that a majority of people in the UK now expect to pay privately for many common treatments [12]. This alone is problematic in the sense of those willing and able to pay purchasing the ability to 'jump the queue' for treatment whilst, at the same time, taking resources in the form of medical time from the publicly funded part of the system where the needs are likely to be greater. The tipping point arises whereby, if enough people are doing this, and the myth continues to be peddled that it relieves pressure on the NHS, such groups are likely to begin to demand tax rebates to support them in their apparently altruistic, but actually selfish, endeavour. This would begin to mimic the Australian health care system, where such inequities, sponsored by government via tax rebates, have been known about for some time [13]. Further political controversies and headaches would arise over the extents to which public hospitals can sell bed space to privately insured patients and to which even private hospitals themselves might receive support from the public purse. Once embarked upon, it would be difficult to reverse such a policy which would only enhance two-tierism and inefficiency; the latter in the sense of less need being met for resources spent on health care.

### *Why Not Hypothecation?*

Hypothecated taxes—that is money collected by taxation for a particular purpose—are often put forward as way of taking the politics out of health care. But, again, if this was the solution, many more governments would have tried it. Inevitably, a tax reserved only for the NHS and/or social care would itself become the subject of great political debate. The recent supplement to National Insurance introduced by the Johnson-led UK Government shows the volatility of such taxes. The supplement was meant to provide the funding for proposals to ease burden on those deemed to be paying too much for social care—more on this in Chapter 3. The main point here is that, due to (it could be argued, self-inflicted) fiscal pressures on the Tory Government, this hypothecated tax was subsequently withdrawn.

### *Why Not Social Insurance?*

We now know that continuous health care reform, often intended to promote greater market discipline, and a constant feature of the NHS throughout its existence, has led to little gain at the cost of significant disruption [4, 5, 14]. So, too, I would predict, with the oft-lauded switch to the social insurance systems of some of our neighbouring countries. Table 2.1 gives a clue as to why such systems might seem to do better than here in the UK; they spend significantly more. This also gives them capacity to focus more on care out of hospital and in general practice; things that have been eroded here in the UK and could be restored without much disruption. The fact that some countries operate social insurance schemes and others taxation-based funding is more a product of history than anything else. The UK had Beveridge, Germany had Bismarck and other countries their versions of the visionaries who helped establish their welfare states in different ways. These systems share more similarities than they have differences. Change from one to the other—whether from an NHS to social insurance or vice versa—would, at best, be futile and, at worst, lead to high costs of disruption.

### *Social Impact Bonds and Private Finance Initiatives: Beware the Chimera of 'Free' Money*

Post-pandemic and just after a cost-of-living crisis, governments across the globe harbour genuine concerns with the optics of asking the public to pay more taxes. Yet, with public services in many countries in disarray post-pandemic, it must be tempting for politicians to seek innovative ways of bringing money into the system in ways that will (at least in appearance) not put pressure on the public purse. A recent development in this regard, post financial crash in 2008, is social impact bonds (SIBs). The rhetoric of SIBs is that private funds, and even dormant banking funds, could be put towards more social uses whilst, at the same time, injecting more of a business culture into funding and performance of public services—surely a win–win?

This would involve the creation of SIBs whereby a service provider, seeking to expand current services or create something new, strikes a deal with a funder that involves: money being paid upfront by a third-party investor; funds flowing, via an intermediary, to providers of the specified service; provision of such funds being tied to goals related, in the health sphere, to health outcomes achieved or improved access for, say, harder-to-reach groups; and, in the event of goals being reached, payments being triggered from the public funder back to the investor, via the intermediary.

However, there are downsides. Although the private funder accepts financial risk of failure, we do not want to be funding failing services anyway. Furthermore, the notion of 'outcome' is really a statistical concept, involving variation, and may not be a good basis for striking contracts. Hence many such SIBs in health, globally, have not specified performance on the basis of such outcomes, which then makes their impacts hard to judge. Finally, in the event of a successful initiative, the money still has to be paid back, and that money comes from the taxpayer. Whole books have been written about this and other types of 'social finance', one of which I have co-authored [15]!

The dangers that lurk are also reminiscent of those of the Private Finance Initiative (PFI), brought in to finance capital developments in the NHS (and elsewhere) whilst keeping the public debt down, but which often tied service providers into quite draconian payback terms which would have been more efficient to fund through public borrowing [16].

It is worth noting that these challenges have been taken on by one of the first health impact bonds in the UK—the 'Ways to Wellness' initiative in Newcastle upon Tyne. The first six years of experience of Ways to Wellness have been reported [17], and refers to a detailed evaluation, led by researchers at Newcastle and Durham Universities and funded by the National Institute of Health Research, but yet to be reported upon. For those interested, it is worth following progress with this development. However, such SIBs are unlikely to be transformative as a basis of funding whole (or substantial parts of) health care systems; if this were to be the case, it would have happened already.

## Conclusion

There are many in government, who, as with other goods once thought to be the preserve of public financing and provision, would divest themselves of the NHS if they could. Experience of recent decades with respect to the stagnation in plans to reform social care would also back up this observation. For the NHS, the reasons they cannot abandon it are due to the nature of health care as a commodity. As early as 1952, the UK Government proposed an enquiry into the cost of the NHS, with a view to dismantling it. This backfired when the subsequent Guillebaud Report of 1956 declared the NHS as value for money.

Despite all health care systems being different in terms of their public–private mix of financing, it is the similarities that are striking; universal coverage is sought and 'insurance' is based on groups rather than private, individual transactions. An added benefit of this is that, by everyone being locked in together, more vulnerable and needier groups benefit from the drive towards higher standards demanded by the vocal middle class, who might otherwise vote for permission to opt out [18]. Rather unusually in this modern world, the key to paying for a better health care system is compulsion not freedom.

The lesson that publicly funded health care is more efficient as well as more equitable has been learned by all countries as they seek to move towards UHC, continuously promoted by the World Health organisation since 1948 and reflected in the Table 2.1 [19]. Aneurin Bevan promoted the establishment of the NHS 'in place of fear' of financial ruin amongst those unfortunate enough to fall sick [1]. He was concerned with fairness and equity. Hopefully, the arguments presented here also show that our current approach to funding the NHS, through taxation, is also more efficient than any alternative. All is not rosy in the NHS, but, with respect to its financing that is, in part, the subject of the rest of this book as well as the expertise of others. The recent LSE-Lancet Commission on the Future of the NHS has shown that modest increases in taxation are the best way to ensure its sustainability (along with social care) going forward [20, 21]. We will return to the cost of sustaining an NHS in Chapter 7 and also need to bear in mind that we could better manage the resources we have, as addressed in Chapter 4. Alongside the challenges of alternatives and to avoid the continuation, indeed spiralling, of our current NHS crisis, our politicians just need to find the courage to explain the virtues of a tax-based system to the public.

## References


1. Bevan A. In Place of Fear. William Heinemann, 1952.
2. Evans RG, Strained Mercy: The Economics of Canadian Health Care. Butterworth, Toronto, 1984.
3. Donaldson C, Gerard K. Economics of Health Care Financing: The Visible Hand. Macmillan, London, 1993.
4. Donaldson C and Gerard K (with Mitton C, Jan S and Wiseman V). Economics of Health Care Financing: The Visible Hand (2nd edition). Palgrave/Macmillan, London, 2005.
5. Donaldson C. Credit Crunch Health Care: How Economics Can Save Our Publicly-Funded Health Services. Policy Press, Bristol, 2011.
6. Adult social care at a glance. National Audit Office, 2018.
7. Woolhandler S and Himmelstein DU. The Deteriorating Administrative Efficiency of the U.S. Health Care System. New England Journal of Medicine 1991; 324: 1253–1258.
8. Woolhandler S, Campbell T and Himmelstein DU. Cost of Health Care Administration in the United States and Canada. New England Journal of Medicine 2003; 349: 768–775.
9. Scottish Government. Independent Review of Adult Social Care in Scotland. 2021.
10. Evans RG. Going for the Gold: The Redistributive Agenda Behind Market-Based Health Care Reform. Journal of Health Politics, Policy and Law 1997; 22: 427–465.
11. Law HD, Marasinghe D, Butler D, Welsh J, Lancsar E, Banks E, Biddle N, Korda R. Progressivity of Out-of-Pocket Costs Under Australia's Universal Health Care System: A National Linked Data Study. Health Policy 2023; 127: 44–50.

12. Davis A, Blackwell C, Ellis E, Padely M, Stone J and Balchin E. A Minimum Income Standard for the United Kingdom in 2024. Joseph Rowntree Foundation, York, 2024. (https://www.jrf.org.uk/a-minimum-income-standard-for-the-united-kingdom-in-2024#about-the-authors).
13. Smith J. How Fair Is Health Spending? The Distribution of Tax Subsidies for Health in Australia. The Australia Institute, Paper Number 43, October 2001. (https://australiainstitute.org.au/wp-content/uploads/2020/12/DP43_8.pdf)
14. Maynard A and Bloor K, Introducing a Market to the United Kingdom's National Health Service. New England Journal of Medicine 1996; 334: 604–608.
15. McHugh N, Biosca O, Donaldson C (2024) Social Finance and Health. Routledge, Abingdon, Oxon.
16. Pollock AM (2006) NHS PLC: The Privatisation of Our Health Care. Verso Books, London.
17. Case T, Drinkwater C, Moffatt S, Bromhead S. Ways to Wellness, the First Six Years: Approach, Findings and Learning, 2021. https://waystowellness.org.uk/site/assets/files/1404/wtw-publication-digital-aug21.pdf.
18. Donaldson C and Bryan S. Compulsion: The Key to Successful US Health Care Reform. Journal of Health Services Research and Policy 2012; 17(2): 106–109.
19. https://www.who.int/news-room/fact-sheets/detail/universal-health-coverage-(uhc).
20. Anderson M, Pitchforth E, Asaria M, Brayne C, Casadei B, Charlesworth A, Coulter A, Franklin BD, Donaldson C, Drummond M, Dunnell KH, Foster M, Hussey R, Johnson P, Knapp M, Lavery G, Longley M, Macleod Clark J, Majeed A, McKee M, Newton J, O'Neill C, Raine R, Richards M, Smith P, Sheikh A, Street A, Taylor D, Watt R, Woods M, Johnston Webber C, McGuire A, Mossialos E. The Future of the NHS: Re-laying the Foundations in a Post COVID-19 World. The Lancet 2021; 397: 1915–1978 (https://www.thelancet.com/journals/lancet/article/PIIS0140-6736(21)00232-4/fulltext).
21. Charlesworth A, Anderson M, Donaldson C, Johnson P, Knapp M, McGuire A, McKee M, Mossialios E, Smith P, Street A, Woods M. The Future of the NHS: What Is the Right Level of Spending Needed for Health and Care in the UK? The Lancet 2021; 397: 2012–2022 (https://doi.org/10.1016/S0140-6736(21)00230-0).

CHAPTER 3

# Resurrecting Demand-Side Socialism: Marching 2 x 2 to Health and Social Care Reform

**Abstract** In this chapter, two separate 2 × 2 analyses are used to examine two issues, these being: the role of the private sector in publicly funded health care systems; and to diagnose and repair the unfairness and inefficiency in adult social care. With respect to the former, by separating out financing (public vs private) from provision (again, public vs private), it can be seen that we might not rule out a role for the private sector in providing care within an NHS-type system. History and evidence support this, the key being that the dominant source of financing, but not necessarily provision, should be public; a form of demand-side socialism. Secondly, by examining social care in terms of its location (either *at* home or *in* a home) and the funding source (public vs self-funding), it is shown that there is a strong case for a system of social care financing similar to that for health care, which in the UK, takes the form of the NHS. It is now recognised that health and social care act in parallel. A well-functioning social care system helps prevent people entering the health care system and also facilitates their earlier discharge. The main policy distraction to be assessed here is that reform of the financing of social care (in the UK) is unaffordable. It would cost very little. Indeed, given the growing number of people with Alzheimer in the social care system, there is an inevitability to the case. There is no reason why the market failure arguments applied to caring for people with other medical conditions, and thus in support of an NHS, should not also apply to this group who just happen to be placed in social care.

© The Author(s), under exclusive license to Springer Nature Switzerland AG 2025

C. Donaldson, *Financing Health and Social Care*,
https://doi.org/10.1007/978-3-031-86769-9_3

**Keywords** Financing vs provision · Private sector · Social care

*When things get complicated, I immediately begin to think about whether I can map out the problem in a diagram on a single page. This often works for me. A particular favourite is a two-by-two (2 × 2) table. Two great examples are used here to help articulate solutions to seemingly intractable issues. The first is a long-standing issue; that of the role of the private sector in health care. The second is more recent, at least in terms of the attention it is receiving; that of social care. The latter, of course, has been an ongoing issue for those at the receiving end of unfair funding arrangements. Let's see if we can help resolve them with our 2 × 2 thinking.*

In April of 2024, then UK Shadow Health Secretary, Wes Streeting, was forced to defend the possibility of using the private sector as part of an initiative to reduce NHS waiting times. On one hand this was seen as a betrayal of Labour values. On the other, as Mr. Streeting said, it can be seen as a pragmatic way to help reduce NHS waiting lists without letting dogma stand in the way of meeting people's health needs in a timely manner.

To many, the very notion of a market in health care is an anathema, or, more politely, a 'contradiction'. A more conciliatory view might be to ask what is the place of markets in our publicly funded systems. Thus, rather than being a contradiction in terms, the phrase 'markets and health care' becomes a conundrum, to be informed not only by evidence but also political history and even future potential. Once we begin to unpick such a policy along each of these lines, Mr. Streeting comes out well, resurrecting the idea of 'demand-side socialism' as a model for the NHS.

The world has learned that equitable as well as efficient health care systems rely on a predomination of public funding, usually via taxation or social insurance [1, 2]. However, this does not preclude competition on the supply side of health care—for example, amongst different providers, such as hospitals, competing for public funds. This demand-side socialism [3] comprises collective funding on the demand side of the health care market, whilst provision (or supply) can be public or private and even involve a degree of competition. My own view is that, to preserve the NHS, the former is a must-do, whilst the latter is more open to question. Here, the concept of demand-side socialism is outlined in more detail before offering a quick review of its history, evidence and future potential as a basis not only for protecting but also advancing the NHS and, later, incorporating social care into a similarly funded system.

## Demand-Side Socialism and the Public–Private Mix of Health Care Financing and Provision

Public financing of health care relates to how the funds are raised, whether through insurance premiums, taxes or whatever. Provision is different, and is more about the institutions through which care is delivered. This is why an apparent contradiction becomes more of a conundrum—there might be scope for markets, or competition, on the provision side, which then requires evidence to establish the degree to which this should occur.

Figure 3.1 illustrates a matrix of cells that represent the combinations of health care financing and provision that can occur. In most advanced economies, the rhetoric is that health services, such as the NHS, are largely publicly financed (as shown earlier in Table 2.1) with no competition in terms of that dimension, as in cell (1).

However, this does not rule out the possibility of competition on the supply side, i.e. amongst providers, such as hospitals, as represented by quadrant (3) alone. As well, referring to this as 'demand-side socialism' [3], we might prefer something pandering to the other end of the political spectrum; 'internal markets'.

The key is that, in terms of the financing of health care, the funds are still public and care remains, largely, free at the point of delivery. This compulsion to participate in funding, via taxation, by locking us all into the one system, ensures that the standards pushed for by the those who are more articulate and less-vulnerable apply to all, and a two-tier (or multi-tier) system is avoided [4]. It also prevents private insurers

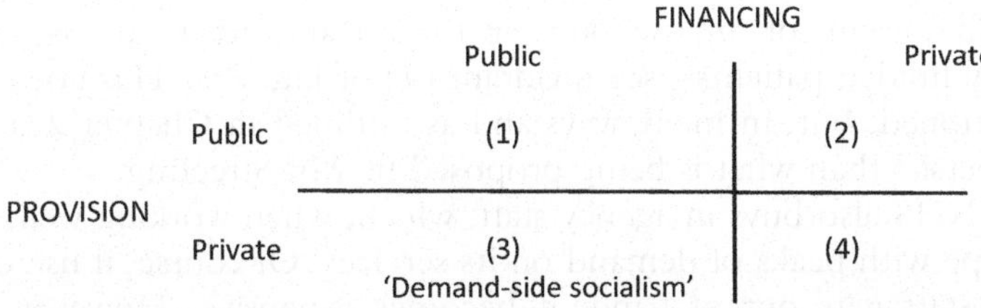


**Fig. 3.1** Public–private mix in health care financing and provision

taking medical time away from the NHS in order to treat less-needy and wealthier patients and ensures that the training we have invested in as a society is used to benefit those on NHS waiting lists as opposed to those who can afford to pay.

None of this is new. Use of public funds to pay for private care goes right back to the origins of the NHS. It also came to the fore during the Thatcher-Clarke UK NHS reforms of the 1990s, commonly known as the internal market. The crucial question then becomes, given that this has happened, what does the evidence say about internal markets, including the role of the private sector within them?

### *History Is on Mr. Streeting's Side*

When we think about it, the part of the NHS with which most people interact is privately provided; that being general practice. Each general practice is a private firm, with owners ('partners'), who, on exit (usually retirement), can sell their stake to new or existing colleagues. It just so happens that the vast majority of general practice activity is publicly funded via the NHS, a situation which also pertains in many countries.

This system has been with us for so long now that we just see general practice as part of the NHS, or of Medicare in countries like Canada and Australia. But it was not always like that. Back in the 1940s, when then UK Health Minister, Aneurin Bevan, was making the case for an NHS, the medical profession was largely opposed. When challenged as to how he would bring the doctors onside, Bevan is famously reported to have said (at a dinner some years later) that 'ultimately, I had to stuff their mouths with gold' [5]. He did, and now over seven decades later, the medical profession is one of the staunchest defenders of the NHS. In addition to general practice, part of their deal was that (predominantly) hospital doctors could supplement their NHS income by spending a limited amount of time working in the private sector; that is, treating privately funded patients—see quadrant (4) of Fig. 3.1. This goes largely unquestioned, but, in many ways and as outlined in Chapter 2, is more controversial than what is being proposed by Mr. Streeting.

The NHS also buys in agency staff, which, when working well, allows it to cope with peaks of demand on its services. Of course, if use of such agency staff gets out of hand, it becomes expensive. However, it has a place. But, such agencies are private businesses. A myriad of arrangements also exist with private providers of allied health services, too, and arrangements with private providers would likely have to occur if social care were brought under a public-funding umbrella, either in the form of an NCS or integrating social care with the NHS; indeed the feasibility of a NCS might be severely called into question with an outright ban on private provision. Also, what is not commonly known is that, within the NHS Choice Framework of NHS England, patients do have the legal right to ask for treatment in a privately owned hospital.

Legislating to ban private provision would likely involve unpicking all of these historical arrangements and, inadvertently, threaten any future potential for greater public funding of social care. Better perhaps to try to make best use of whatever capacity is there in the private system. If such capacity exists, then contracts for care, funded by the NHS, could be negotiated at the marginal cost of provision, which somewhat negates arguments that the price of such provision includes profit. To explain, NHS tariffs are based on average costs which have to cover all resources such as staffing and capital costs. The origins of such tariffs go back to the introduction of diagnosis related groups (DRGs) into the US Medicare system in the 1980s as one way to control costs. Similarly, NHS tariffs differ by diagnosis, but, like DRGs, are essentially averages. If there is *existing spare capacity* in private hospitals, then the additional (marginal) costs of admitting a few NHS-funded patients will not be as much as the average because, without such admissions, capital and staffing costs would still have to be met. This gives the NHS considerable scope for negotiation on price. But, note, this is only where there is *existing spare capacity*. A different scenario arises if the NHS was paying full (average-based) rates for actual expansions in private hospital bed capacity, which would then involve coverage of capital costs (e.g. buildings and equipment) as well as staff, a much more expensive proposition against which legitimate claims could be made that expanding public provision would be better.

### *Evidence Is on Mr. Streeting's Side (for Health But Not Social Care)*

In the 1990s, early adopters of internal markets were the UK, New Zealand and Sweden, but versions now exist in several countries. Briefly, money allocated from central government goes into the hands of geographically defined 'health authorities' (HAs), as in the previously existing systems in these countries. However, rather than just passively allocating the money to historically provided services, under internal markets, providers had to compete to win contracts from HAs. Through competition amongst providers, the aim was to improve quality and reduce costs, not only of medical care but also other services provided through hospitals, whether public or private. So, what Mr. Streeting is proposing has been legislated for some time. Indeed, it could be argued that it should go further with the NHS flexing more of its collective buying power as regards procurement.

Generally, however, opportunities for such competition were counterbalanced by several things. These included directives from 'the centre', crude contracting mechanisms (which meant that large amounts of money were simply handed over to providers as in the old system), the enormity of the task and a general risk-aversion amongst HAs with respect to not wanting to destabilise a local provider by moving some finance from it to some other provider. Where any such destabilisation occurred, the tendency was to resort to Government-based solutions, as illustrated in London in 1991 [6]. Almost immediately after the internal market was introduced, HAs on the outskirts of the capital shifted resources out of relatively expensive central London hospitals to those in less-costly and more-accessible surrounding areas. This threatened the sustainability of some (prestigious) central London hospitals. The internal market in London was suspended and a review of health services in the UK capital, led by Sir Bernard Tomlinson, undertaken. Overall, doubt has been cast on the impact of such reforms, with small gains in outcomes achieved at the expense of higher administrative and contracting costs and also whilst more cash was being injected into the system anyway; making it difficult to separate the impacts of the reforms from that of the extra funds [7].

On the specific question of the cost-effectiveness of public versus private providers operating in a publicly funded health care system, like the NHS, there is no published evidence. The focus of the literature tends to be on the for-profit versus not-for-profit hospital literature. Rather than select articles and reports to help make the case for one side or other of this controversial debate, one systematic review of the literature, from Canada, was undertaken in order to provide a balanced view of the evidence [8]. Thirty-four studies were identified and most of these found no difference between for-profit and not-for-profit full-service hospitals with respect to relative costs, quality of care or efficiency—a conclusion that is contrary to the more selective reviews which focus on the results from either favourable or unfavourable studies, depending on whether or not one promotes for-profit provision. It is also a conclusion backed up by more-recent reviews [9]. There are some studies which review the impact of hospitals converting from being public to private [10]. However, this also does not specifically address the question which Mr. Streeting might be considering, which is "What are the costs, risks and benefits of using existing private sector capacity to help relieve NHS waiting lists?" Despite a call for more research with respect to regulation and risk assessment in public–private partnerships more generally in the health sector [11], this has not been heeded.

Recent evidence on social care is somewhat different. Regulatory authorities collect much data on quality of care homes, such as safety, effectiveness and meeting needs. Comprehensive analyses using such data has shown that for-profit homes perform worse than their public sector or not-for-profit (third sector) counterparts [12, 13]. This presents a further challenge for the reform of social care which we discuss in the following section.

### *The Future Evolution of Healthcare Is on Mr. Streeting's Side*

At this juncture it is also worth considering how the NHS and other health care systems around the globe will cope with the three intertwining forces of artificial intelligence and robotics, omics and our ability to engineer human biology, and the application of systems science to healthcare. Indeed, we are now (some would say, once again) being promised a digital revolution in the NHS. But, can this be done without involving private providers? If not, then the key is to achieve this and still within the confines of demand-side socialism, i.e. to the benefit of all within a publicly funded system.

It could be argued that the only way to bring about the scale and pace of transformation required in the NHS is through the market entry of private companies with a proven track record of industry disruption in the same way that Amazon disrupted and completely transformed first book selling, then the entire retail market, or that Apple disrupted and transformed the music industry with the iPod and iTunes. These so-called tech titans were able to achieve such radical transformations of old established industries because they were unencumbered by historical precedent; they re-imagined, then re-designed systems and processes using technology, and in so doing realised enormous improvements in quality of service and efficiency. Apple has already signalled its strategic intent to enter the healthcare market through key partnerships with the Mayo Clinic, the University of Pittsburgh Medical Center, and Johnson & Johnson, and through acquisitions of healthcare companies [14]. Amazon has made a more direct foray into healthcare provision through its acquisition of the boutique US primary health care chain, One Medical, and offering discounted healthcare subscriptions to its Amazon Prime members [15].

Perhaps a relevant analogy to the challenge facing a largely publicly provided NHS, is the disruption of the UK's television entertainment industry by the next generation of technology disruptors, led by Netflix. One might argue that in the UK, Netflix (and its competitors) is able to offer a service to the British public that provides more value for money than the 'publicly provided' BBC. Given the direction Amazon has taken in the US, it's not a long stretch to imagine such services being bundled with preventive and primary health care offerings, but publicly funded here in the UK, and perhaps branded as 'part of the NHS family'. The logical next step would be for such companies to further integrate primary and secondary care delivery, including the acquisition of hospitals, or the creation of completely new kinds of health care settings. Apple provides another pertinent analogy, with its successful integration with, and re-imagining of, computer retailing in the shape of the Apple Store.

To recap, and in short, they key is to retain public funding, whilst unpacking the idea of who is a legitimate provider of care—public, private or even some hybrid—without jeopardising the current system as well as its future progress. This latter point applies to social care to which we now turn.

## Saving (Adult) Social Care

For many years, care home residents and their relatives in the UK have persevered with adverse user experiences alongside rising care costs with limited financial support. This has led to considerable anxiety, uncertainty and financial stress. So much so that, in 2011, the Commission on Funding of Care and Support, chaired by economist Andrew Dilnot, reported on potential reforms to support people using care services in England [16]. Dilnot was never enacted, which is an instructive example of how Western Governments, and no doubt others around the globe, have struggled with this issue.

The purpose of the reminder of this chapter, therefore, is not only to illustrate the potential nature and brutality of care home funding systems, the contention being that this is the current situation in Scotland and England, but also to propose reasonable (costed) alternatives for funding care which would be fairer and also more efficient. It also shows the dangers of moving to more mixed models of funding and provision for health care. The more mixed, and messy, it gets, the more potential for exploitation for profit to the detriment of meeting need.

### *Care Funding: Who Cares? Who Pays?*

As with health care, all countries have different methods of funding community-based health care and their care home systems. To analyse such systems would be impossible, as the subtleties are more complex than for health care. The systems around the countries of the UK are broadly similar. Internationally, too, most advanced economies operate systems which combine public and private funding with provision which can be for-profit, not-for-profit or private [17]. A useful way to aid analysis of the efficiency and equity of any system in any country is to construct a simple framework of the sort you can see can see in our next 2 × 2, Fig. 3.2. Here, for purposes of generalisability, an attempt has been made to set out a system in as generic a way as possible. However, to also add a degree of reality, and help illustrate some of the points to be made, reference will be made to the systems across the UK and especially that in Scotland.

Returning to Fig. 3.2, our generic system is outlined according to whether any given client is in receipt of care at home or care in a home (who cares) and also whether that care is publicly funded or self-funded (who pays). Quadrants (1) and (2) represent the situation for those cared for at home. From a 'who pays' perspective, these groups are often less problematic. Issues are mainly about levels of service provided, especially so in the case of quadrant (1). Many in quadrant (2) will also be wealthy enough or make use of additional benefits to carers (jn the UK, Attendance Allowance) to bridge the gap between the help they receive from family and informal carers and what they are allocated by the State. However, some in quadrant (2) may lie somewhere in-between.

There have been calls in some countries to remove charges for non-residential support services [18], effectively rendering all care at home (personal and non-personal) free. The argument for this is prevention (e.g. of escalation of a condition and hospital admission) and that it removes barriers to person-centred services: charges distort choices and result in unmet need (people with eligible needs refusing to take up services due to charges), and unmet need in due course can result in accelerated needs and higher care costs in future [19]. The argument against

| FUNDING SOURCE | LOCATION OF CARE: Home care | LOCATION OF CARE: Care home |
|---|---|---|
| **Publicly-funded** | (1)<br>All nursing and personal care is free for people assessed as having eligible needs.<br>Providers might be public or private.<br>The cost will depend on the needs of the individual and there is no limit.<br>Domiciliary social care services falling outside the definition of personal care ((e.g. housework, food, laundry etc.) and services outside of the home (e.g. lunch clubs, transport) could be free but are often means tested and charged accordingly. | (3)<br>Eligibility for public funding is often based on having capital assets (e.g. a privately-owned home, money in the bank) less than some defined threshold.<br>On 'qualifying' for public funding, limits would then be placed on entitlements – so much for nursing care and so much for residential care. Rather than a single defined threshold, a gradient may be employed whereby, as wealth levels grow, the public contribution would proportionately diminish.<br>Also, to help with funding, a person's State, and even occupational pensions, may be taken from them, with a small amount retained for 'pocket money'. |
| **Self-funded** | As above, except that people are often free to choose to pay private for more or alternative personal and domiciliary social care services.<br>(2) | As with quadrant (2), people would be free to 'opt out and go totally private.<br>However, some entitlement to public subsidy for personal and nursing care might exist.<br>Again, to help with funding, carers' allowances would likely be transferred to the nursing home.<br>With many being private businesses, care homes are free to set their own prices/charges.<br>(4) |

**Fig. 3.2** Social care: who cares? Who pays? *Note* Between quadrants (3) and (4) there is a third categorisation—transitional group—comprising those whose capital is inaccessible (e.g. locked up in a house) which means that the local authority covers most of their costs, but the individuals contribute via a charge levied by the local authority. The arrangements are similar as for quadrant (3), with the addition of a payment to the local authority based on 'charging rules' related to the amount of capital locked up

is the financial risk in not being able to quantify the cost of the additional demand when charges are removed particularly if care is no longer defined as a limited series of tasks but includes the relational aspects of caring.

Focusing more on quadrants (3) and (4), due to that being more of a current issue in the UK, on the face of it, it might seem that the system as characterised is reasonable and fair. Those in the less-well-off-group, occupying quadrant (3), are the ones in receipt of greater amounts of public funding towards their care. However, the key issues, in any system will be to do with the thresholds and levels of support set by government. If we get these wrong, then it could lead to those in quadrant (4) becoming more attractive propositions for care homes to take in, leading to two gross inequities; not only the de-prioritising of those on lower incomes in quadrant (3) but also an unfair financial burden placed on those in quadrant (4), who we have labelled 'self-funders', who often happen to be only a little better off than those in quadrant (3).

To address the anxieties and distress caused by such potential injustices, as long ago as 2011, the Commission on Funding of Care and Support, chaired by economist Andrew Dilnot, reported on potential reforms to support people using care services in England [16]. Dilnot was never enacted, and further promises, such as the Johnson Government's proposed Health and Social Care Levy, have been abandoned. (Incidentally, as well as being a good example of a hypothecated tax, the Levy also provides an excellent demonstration of how such taxes can be taken away almost as soon as they have been introduced.) This was never going to be enough, especially as the majority of the funds raised were promised to the NHS and not social care anyway. Meanwhile, in Scotland, a policy of free personal and nursing care (FPNC) has been in place since 2002. Reference to this policy in Scotland is often made; giving the impression that this issue has been resolved north of the border. However, this is not the case. The Scottish model has also been proposed recently as a possible way forward in England [20].

To illustrate, it is necessary to get into the details of particular countries. What determines who is publicly funded or a self-funder in Scotland and England is outlined in Table 3.1 and compared with what Dilnot proposed. There are some subtleties (in the notes) with respect to out-of-pocket payments and deferrals of payment based on property sales that may exist for some residents. It can be seen that people are disqualified from support from the state at quite low levels of wealth and, currently, no limits are placed on out-of-pocket costs for which care home residents are liable; these being paralleled in England and also being two of the main issues Dilnot sought to repair.

**Table 3.1** Care home funding: Dilnot vs England vs Scotland

| | *Scotland (as of 2024)* | *England* | *Dilnot (2011)* |
|---|---|---|---|
| Means testing, such that state support is available for those with assets below a threshold of...[a] | £21,500-£35,000[b] | £14,250–23,250[b] | £100,000 |
| Limit on lifetime care home out-of-pocket contributions for personal and nursing care only, i.e. not 'hotel' costs | No limit | No limit[c] | £25,000–50,000 (£35,000 considered fair) |

[a]For those below this threshold, some out-of-pocket payments may still apply. If sole-owner of a property and/or living alone, the value of the property is taken into account. Deferrals of payment, from a later sale of a property, are possible

[b]For those between lower and upper limits, out-of-pocket contributions (less than the self-funding rate) are made, calculated via a formula

[c]A cap of £86,000 has recently been proposed for introduction in England in 2025, but since abandoned by the newly elected Labour Government

To illustrate further, most people who need to reside in a care home in Scotland who have more than the capital limits (between £21,500 and £35,000 including the value of their home and any savings) are in practice advised they need to arrange and pay their own care home costs. (The original guidance on Free Personal and Nursing Care, which has never been withdrawn, advised that self-funders should be able to choose to come under what is now the National Care Home Contract and pay local authority rates but that has effectively been abandoned [21]). Take, for example a (representative) care home at the upper end of the market requiring a large deposit and total payment of £1705 a week. The care home will collect the personal care and nursing care allowances paid by the local authority (the 'free' part) directly; a total of £360.60 per week (£248.70 for personal care and £111.90 for nursing care). Note also that, on entering care, Attendance Allowance (currently £108.55 a week and paid to carers, usually a relative) is lost, effectively cancelling out the nursing care element. Nevertheless, effectively, a 'self-funder' in that care home is worth £88,660 (£1705 × 52) in revenue per annum. Crucially, for the case to be made, the shortfall between the full rate and the free part (£1705–338 = £1367) is made up of £251pw, for care which is meant to be free, plus another £1116pw in 'hotel' costs.

However, when people who have less than the capital limit are placed in care, it is arranged and funded by their local authority at rates agreed annually in the National Care Home Contract (NCHC) between CoSLA (the Convention of Scottish Local Authorities, the representative body for local government in Scotland), Scottish Care and the Coalition of Care Providers Scotland (CCPS). These rates from April 2023 are £948.59 per week for nursing care and £825.94 per week for residential care. (Please note this is not a net figure for local authority payments—local authorities will actually contribute considerably less, as everything a person receives in State and Occupational Pensions is taken from them, except £34.50 per week 'pocket money'.) Even so, the upshot is that a publicly funded person in a nursing home is worth £43,576 in revenue, about half the rate of self-funders even if they are in the same care home, living under exactly the same conditions and in receipt of more-generous amounts of public funding.

The justification for the high charges to self-funders is two-fold. Firstly, that the NCHC rates, although supposedly designed to cover all costs plus a return, do not do so and the higher rates that are charged to self-funders are necessary to subsidise the cost of caring for publicly funded residents. For example, claims were made to the Independent Review of Adult Social Care that a number of providers have now built a business model based on using private rates to subsidise local authority rates. Whilst doubtful that a single Scotland-wide NCHC rate adequately covers the actual cost of care provision, at least in some geographies, other evidence suggests the 'need to subsidise publicly-funded residents' justification is largely a myth. For example, there is no evidence that care homes with high charges actually pay their staff more than the Scottish Living Wage, on which the NCHC rates are based, whilst there are some private care homes, including *HC-One*, which primarily offer care to people who are publicly funded and remain profitable. Whilst the steep decline in not-for-profit care homes is often taken to indicate that the NCHC rate is not keeping pace with actual costs [22], the explanation is far more complex. Whilst a commitment to pay staff more than the living wage may have forced some out of business, changes in ideology which favoured care in the community and the ability of the private sector to access capital to replace old buildings have been very important. The associated reduction in both voluntary sector and local authority care home places has left self-funders even more exposed to the profit-taking private market.

Secondly, there is the argument that some providers are offering facilities and services significantly above those required by National Care Standards. The Scottish Government's guidance on free personal and nursing care allowed providers to charge for such services and facilities, but there has been no research to quantify the actual cost of providing these. What we do know from various reports into the care home market is that care home charging is far from transparent and that there are serious questions about the fairness of charges for extra services and facilities [23, 24].

### *Resulting Incentives and Consequent Inequities: Are We Throwing People to the Wolves?*

From a private provider perspective, the less-generous scenario with respect to receipt of public funds and lack of controls over what they can charge means care homes are incentivised to attract self-funders. Correspondingly, there is a reluctance from many providers to accept publicly funded residents. Increasingly, this is creating a two-tier care system, recent evidence, from England, having shown that there is a growing concentration of care homes in more-affluent areas and greater rates of closure in more-deprived areas [25, 26]

Meanwhile, at the level of the wider health and social care system, publicly funded people often have to wait longer for a vacancy whilst relatives of self-funders delay as long as they can as they adjust to the shock of the costs they will now face when their loved-one leaves the hospital setting; each contributing to bed-blocking in many hospitals.

Turning to communities, it is not unreasonable to think of a self-funding older person entering the care home system who has been living alone after the death of their partner, who has paid for their house and/or received a lump sum on retirement and, if surviving for a reasonable amount of time, literally having to give up 100% of all they (and their spouse) have accumulated over a lifetime. Relatives will also be making decisions and signing contracts at a very stressful time, many with no idea of what will happen when the money runs out. With an average house price in Scotland (at May 2023) of £192,000 and a mean length of stay (LoS) in a care home of 2.2 years, for many (above the mean LoS and/or with property valued below the mean price), their money could run out in three years, if not before. With 70% of the elderly care home population female, this could be seen as a raid on the wealth of older women in particular [27].

The threat to self-funders arises from two sources: having to pay some of their care costs where policy is that it should be free; and having to pay their hotel costs. Government is committed to making up the first shortfall, but is not doing so. The second is more open to debate as to what might happen. Dilnot was not proposing to cover hotel costs [16]. This situation is further compounded by the lack of control over care home charges. It used to be that a 'blind eye' was turned to homes charging 'self-funders' a little more than the LA rate. The gap between what the LA 'pays' (remembering that some of what the LA pays is reimbursed from reduced allowances elsewhere) and what self-funders pay has grown 3–fourfold since the introduction of free personal and nursing care.

Growing numbers of people, without exposure to expert financial planning or generous occupational pensions, are having to fund all their care costs (bar the personal care allowance) from basic state pension plus the capital return on the sale of the family home. Recent cases, presenting to Care Home Relatives Scotland during 2023, illustrate such situations—see Cases 1 and 2 in Box 3.1. The third case shows that it is sometimes possible to negotiate a 'deal' with a care home, which points to the possibility of systematising the care home commitment to its residents, regardless of funding source rather than relying on individuals having the knowledge and confidence to seek such an agreement. In a modification to the Care Act of 2014, such an initiative, giving self-funders the right to request the LA to arrange their care, is to be introduced in England in 2025 [28].

**Box 3.1 Examples from Care Home Relatives Scotland, 2023**

*Case 1: Evicted from a care home*

One member was ordered by a major care provider to take her mother out of a home where she had already spent £250,000 because the home refused to accept the local authority rate to which the mother was now being transferred due to her assets having been run-down so that she no longer qualified as a self-funder.

*Case 2: Alzheimer's.*

Alzheimer's Scotland are finding relatives being asked to find the difference and struggling to do this. Indeed, two further members of Care Home Relatives Scotland, with two parents in care with Alzheimer's have handed over more than £500,000 to care homes in recent years.

*Case 3: Negotiating the 'market'*

Another member, when placing her mother in care, obtained a letter from the company confirming that, when her mother's resources were depleted, the home would accept the local authority fee. But, not all are able to negotiate the market in such an informed way.

The increasing number of self-funders, and consequent growth in exposures to such financial risk, are further shown by Scottish Government's own figures. In 2011, 9113 of care home residents (28%) were self-funders whilst 23,432 (72%) were publicly funded. By 2023/204, it is estimated that 11,691 (35%) will be self-funded, with 19,309 (62%) publicly funded, in part caused by capital limits not keeping pace with asset inflation but also a reflection of increasing levels of home ownership amongst older people since Margaret Thatcher introduced the right to buy council houses. It is also the case that, of those publicly funded, we do not know how many were previously self-funded and whose money has run out.

It is the former council house owners who have been squeezed most by the increase in fees for self-funders and the capital limits the proportion of savings they face losing is far higher than people who own homes at the top end of the market. This risk of financial hardship is continuously growing and, with the associated likelihood of leaving people penniless quicker, the public sector is exposed to growing risks of incurring substantial costs in the future.

### *Back to Market Failure: Demand-Side Socialism in Social Care*

Redistribution, from those able to pay to those less able to pay, is often thought desirable in the context of public services, particularly in the case of health care throughout advanced economies [29]. However, this is generally achieved through the taxation system, so distributing resources from rich to poor and from those more fortunate not to have to use services at all to those who do, not through private markets. As discussed in detail in Chapter 2, this is the well-recognised basis of funding of the UK's NHS, and the health care systems of many other countries. In no other part of society does this allegedly require one group of service users subsidising the other; the 'tax' rate for contributors amounting to 100% of their assets should they be fortunate (or unfortunate) to live long enough. For a group of people who are not wealthy by any reasonable measure, Scotland could be seen as imposing one of the most regressive forms of 'tax' ever invented.

Dementia and other long-term conditions present a particularly interesting challenge. Just over 60% of care home residents in Scotland have dementia, with prevalence projected to increase by 40% over the next 20 years [30]. There is a strong case for their needs being defined as health care needs, especially for those in more-advanced stages of the condition. Similar cases can be made for many other neurological conditions including Motor Neuron Disease, advanced Parkinson's, head injuries and severe strokes. Indeed, the conditions required to support such cases are exactly the same as those outlined in support of public funding of the NHS and similar such health care systems around the globe [29], arguments which were extended recently in support of a publicly funded NCS [31]. The implication is that the associated costs of meeting such needs be met in full from the public purse, so alleviating people not only from having to cope with the diagnosis in and of itself but also the costs of care required to manage the condition. Abandoning such people to the laws of market forces, even if partially subsidised by taxpayers, should not happen for a condition of such gravity. It should also be noted that many people enter care homes because they need palliative care for end of life which would previously have been provided in long stay NHS facilities.

### *Where Now? In Place of Fear in Social Care*

For two decades the myth of free personal care has been peddled in Scotland. Not only is this untrue. It also covers up gross injustices with respect to financial contributions and distress as well as well as contributing to the severest of pressures on the NHS; that of bed-blocking.

The recent Health Foundation report supports the case for a fairer system and its cost being relatively affordable [2]. Step 1, is to enact all care at home to be free, the cost of this having been estimated to amount to at least £51 m (or £9.33 per head) per annum [18].

For care homes, there are three further concrete steps towards an affordable and fairer system, as outlined in Steps 2 and 4 in Table 3.2, all eliminating the perverse incentives contributing to injustices and inefficiencies.

Step 2 involves public coverage of care costs in care homes for all based on national pay rates for staff similar to Agenda for Change in the NHS. This would require an accompanying uplift in the NCHC rate to ensure full-cost coverage for those publicly funded; this would remove the main justification for charging self-funders more, the alleged need to subsidise those who are publicly funded.

**Table 3.2** Towards full-integrated publicly funded care

| | *Estimated cost* | *Cost per capita [and per taxpayer]* |
|---|---|---|
| *Step 1*<br>All care at home to be free | This was estimated at £51 m pa by the Independent Review of Adult Social Care [18] | £9.33 [£19.11][a] |
| *Step 2*<br>Contributions by LAs towards FPNC otherwise paid by self-funders be increased to match levels included in the National Care Home Contract | Also estimated by the Independent Review of Adult Social Care, at £146 m pa [18] | £26.86 [£55.72][a] |
| *Step 4*<br>Meet health care (or full) costs of people with dementia | Cost of £49 m (£123 m) pa estimated by Alzheimer Scotland | £9.01 (£22.62) [£18.36 (£46.10)][a] |
| Total costs per head (taxpayer) | | £45.25–54.60 [£93.19–120.93] |

[a]Cost per capita and per taxpayer based on estimated Scottish population of 5,436,600 (2022 Census) and 2,667,700 taxpayers in tax year 2021–2022

Step 3 would be about implementing effective controls about what care home providers can charge for hotel costs through contracts and better regulation. This would have no costs to the public purse and would only limit profit levels. Without such controls, any increased public funding for care costs would, as when free personal and care payments were first reduced, simply result in hikes to care fees. Where providers decided to leave the market because of limits on profits services could be insourced [32].

Step 4 would address residents with dementia and similar neurological disorders, which we would see as requiring full coverage of costs similar to treating such people as though they were in receipt of care through the NHS. Indeed, if the supply of care home places remains static, then, given projected increases in numbers of residents with dementia, this proposal might result in full (care and 'hotel') costs being covered by the public purse anyway.

Cost estimates for steps 1 and 3 are provided by others [27, 30], with estimated burdens on the population and on taxpayers being merely indicative. Estimates for step 4 will also likely overlap with those for step 1. But, treating the two steps as additive for now, the total amounts to £35–55 per annum per capita; or around £1 per week per head of population. If translated into burdens on Scottish taxpayers, this would amount to around £93–121 per annum, or just over £2 per week. Based on the average wage in Scotland, this would add around 2% to the combined income tax and National Insurance bill, 3% to income tax alone. The social costs would be less due to savings made by current self-funders. These steps could also be accompanied by a commitment of LAs to care for residents in situ, although incentives to move people out once they are unable to pay out-of-pocket would be greatly diminished.

Left open are considerations of what to do about hotel charges (for non-dementia residents) within care homes and the contributions that residents could, more justly, be asked to make towards this from both income and capital. It is worth noting, however, that the Scottish Government has the power to vary both the personal allowance and capital limits under the National Assistance Regulations and those powers could be used to ensure those with limited amounts of capital could not be deprived of this through hotel costs whilst the contributions of those with greater capital kept pace with changes in property prices.

## Conclusions

The key to maintaining an NHS in the long-run is public funding. It is not necessarily contradictory to introduce market forces on the provider side of health care markets. The context into which market forces are introduced is crucial to the discussion. This has happened throughout the history of the NHS. The evidence base, though patchy, is, if anything slightly favourable. Social care is different, as, in that sector, we are coming from a situation in which the market forces have had too much influence. Following the establishment of the NHS in place of fear of financial ruin amongst those unfortunate enough to fall sick [33], the costs of doing the same for social care would seem a small price to pay in place of fear for those unfortunate enough to require care at home or admission to a care home. Hopefully, the reader can make use of our 2 × 2 analyses to help not only understand but help resolve these issues in ways that do not distract us from the great potential in a new and revitalised demand-side socialism, best serving the needs of our populations through sustainable and high-performing health and social care systems at the forefront of the coming revolution in health care and going well beyond the centenary of the NHS.

## References

1. Evans RG, Strained Mercy: the Economics of Canadian Health Care. Butterworth, Toronto, 1984.
2. Donaldson C. Credit Crunch Health Care: How Economics Can Save Our Publicly-Funded Health Services. Policy Press, Bristol, 2011.
3. Culyer AJ. The Normative Economics of Health Care Finance and Provision. In McGuire A, Fenn P and Mayhew K (eds) Providing Health Care: The Economics of Alternative Systems of Finance and Delivery. Oxford University Press, Oxford, 1991.
4. Donaldson C and Bryan S. Compulsion: The Key to Successful US Health Care Reform. Journal of Health Services Research and Policy 2012; 17(2): 106–109.
5. Webster C (ed). Aneurin Bevan on the National Health Service. University of Oxford, Wellcome Unit for the History of Medicine, 1991.
6. Ham C. Public, Private or Community: What Next for the NHS? Demos, London, 1996.
7. Maynard A and Bloor K. Introducing a Market to the United Kingdom's National Health Service. New England Journal of Medicine 1996; 334: 604–608.

8. Currie G, Donaldson C and Lu M. What Does Canada Profit from the for-profit Debate? Canadian Public Policy 2003; 29: 227–251.
9. Tynkkynen L-K and Vrangbaek K. Comparing Public and Private Providers: A Scoping Review of Hospital Services in Europe. BMC Health Services Research 2018; 18: 141 https://doi.org/10.1186/s12913-018-2953-9.
10. Goodair B and Reeves A. The Effect of Health Care Privatisation on Quality of Care. Lancet Public Health 2024; 9: e199–206.
11. Torchia M, Calabro A, Morner M. Public-Private Partnerships in the Health Care Sector: a Systematic Review of the Literature. Public Management Review 2015; 17(2): 236–261 https://doi.org/10.1080/14719037.2013.792380
12. Barron DN and West E. The Quasi-Market for Adult Residential Care in the UK: Do for-profit and Not-For-Profit Public Sector Residential Care and Nursing Homes Provide Better Quality of Care? Social Science and Medicine 2017; 179: 137–146.
13. Patwardhan S, Sutton M, Morciano M. Effects of Chain Ownership and Private Equity Financing on Quality of Care in English Care Home Sector: Retrospective Observational Study. Age and Ageing 2022; 51 (12): afac222 https://doi.org/10.1093/ageing/afac222.
14. https://www.healthcare.digital/single-post/apple-s-healthcare-strategy-build-buy-or-partner-buy-appears-to-be-the-most-likely.
15. https://www.npr.org/2023/11/12/1212534782/amazon-is-getting-into-health-care-will-it-actually-make-care-more-accessible.
16. Dilnot A. Fairer Care Funding: Report of the Commission on Funding of Care and Support. HMSO, London, 2011.
17. Goodair B, Esposti MD and Bach-Mortensen A. How Outsourcing Has Contributed to England's Social Care Crisis. BMJ 2024; 387: 193–197.
18. Scottish Government. Independent Review of Adult Social Care in Scotland. 2021.
19. Tamblyn R, Laprise R, Hanley JA, Abrahamowicz M, Scott S, Mayo N, Hurley J, Grad R, Latimer E, Perrault R, McLeod P, Huang A, Larochelle P and Mallet L. Adverse Effects Associated with Prescription Drug Cost-Sharing Among Poor and Elderly Persons. Journal of the American Medical Association 2001; 285: 2328–2329.
20. Social Care Reform in England. Choices for the Next Government. Health Foundation, 23rd January 2024 (Social Care Funding Reform in England - The Health Foundation).
21. Scottish Executive. Free Personal and Nursing Care – Consolidated Guidance, CCD5/2003
22. https://www.publichealthscotland.scot/media/19501/2022-09-13-care-home-census-report-v10.pdf #page14 and 28.

23. Competition and Markets Authority. Care Home Markets Study, Final Report. 2017.
24. Office of Fair Trading. Care Homes for Older People in the UK. 2005.
25. Bach-Mortensen A, Barlow J, Walker CC, Goodair B, Esposti MD. Evidencing the Outsourcing of Social Care Provision in England. Nuffield Trust, London, 2024.
26. Bach-Mortensen A, Goodair B, Esposti MD. Evidencing the Outsourcing of Social Care Provision in England. Does Outsourcing Enable Survival of Good Care Homes? A Longitudinal Analysis of All Care Homes in England 2011–2023. BMJ Public Health 2024; 2: e001227.https://doi.org/10.1136/bmjph-2024-001227.
27. Independent Review of Adult Social Care in Scotland. Core Brief – Care Home Managed Market, 16th December 2021.
28. Build Back Better: Our Plan for Healthcare. Cabinet Office, Department of Health and Social Care and Prime Minister's Office, 2022.
29. Donaldson C. Credit Crunch Health Care: How Economics Can Save Our Publicly-Funded Systems. Policy Press, Bristol, 2011.
30. Alzheimer Scotland. Delivering Fair Dementia Care for People With Advanced Dementia. The Fair Dementia Care Commission, 2019.
31. Donaldson C. The economic case for a National Care Service. BMJ Opinion (https://blogs.bmj.com/bmj/2021/04/16/cam-donaldson-covid-19-and-the-economic-case-for-a-national-care-service/).
32. Mudd, A. Towards a Real National Care Service for Scotland. APSE/Unison Scotland, 2023.
33. Bevan A. In Place of Fear. William Heinemann, 1952.

CHAPTER 4

# The Fiscal Management of Health and Social Care

**Abstract** The *quid pro quo* for a public system is that claims on such systems will always outstrip the resources we have available to put into them. Here, the main principles behind an economic approach to managing such scarcity are outlined, along with some short case studies of using these in practice. Some important policy distractions also require addressing. For example, does having national-level health technology assessment (HTA) agencies really address the issue of scarcity? How do we know HTA agencies have made our health care systems more efficient? The idea, here, is that we need to get further into localities in combination with national-level HTA. There are also many management frameworks, such as lean thinking and balanced scorecards, that take on the appearance of solving issues of resource scarcity, but without facing up the real choices that have to be made. We have to avoid health and social care managers constantly succumbing to such gimmicks; but part of this involves making the health economics frameworks work for them.

**Keywords** Priority setting · Programme Budgeting and Marginal Analysis (PBMA) · Efficiency · Lean thinking · Opportunity cost · Health Technology Assessment (HTA)

© The Author(s), under exclusive license to Springer Nature Switzerland AG 2025

C. Donaldson, *Financing Health and Social Care*,
https://doi.org/10.1007/978-3-031-86769-9_4

*If you stopped to read about me at the beginning of this book, you will see I have moved around a lot. Each job brings new responsibilities. To accommodate these, it is worth thinking about what to drop. For my later moves, I have thought about trying to drop the research area outlined in this chapter—basically, that of developing and applying economics-based frameworks for more localised priority setting. But, each time I fail. The reason for this is that, every time there is a reform of the health care system, managers of the newly created entities come knocking because they realise that they are still faced with more claims on their resources than they can fund from their allocated budgets. Public funding and health care reform do not eliminate scarcity of resources. This has now become the one permanence in my work life, working with (mostly) health care managers who have to deal with scarcity on a daily basis. They are amazing people, and that's why I can never say 'no!'.*

Let us present this chapter in reverse and start with three common placebos. The first is that, once we have decided that health (and social) care should be publicly funded, then all reasonable claims on resources can be met. The second is that, when reality dawns, and we realise that there are not enough resources to meet all such claims—which often takes the form of a funding crisis—the solution always seems to be to 'reform' the system. Indeed, this is happening right now in health and social care, with talk of the need to reform the 'broken' system because no new money is available. Third, and it might seem contradictory for a health economist to be saying this, is the myth that creation of a national-level health technology assessment solves the issue of the need to judge value for money and, on that basis, set priorities. There are many other gimmicks that pop up from time to time—do people remember the balanced scorecard?- occupying managers' time during times of crisis, but doing little to address the fundamental problem of recognising and managing scarcity.

We will return to each of these proposed 'solutions' in slightly more detail shortly. What they will show is that the NHS (and now social care) has never really faced up to the issue of scarcity management despite several funding crises. Things may seem bad now, but the first funding crisis for the NHS arose in the early 1950s, when the Guillebaud Report concluded that the NHS was indeed value for money. Some might even refer to the work of a young Brian Abel-Smith of the National Institute for Economic and Social Research (and subsequently LSE), the economist on this Commission, as the birth of health economics in the UK [1].

There have been subsequent crises since, where morale is always reported as the worst it has ever been. The most recent, prior to now, was that following the global financial crisis of 2008, when the prospect of 20–30% cuts in the NHS budget loomed.

Thus, almost since the inception of the NHS, there have been debates about its sustainability as well about how to set priorities across the competing claims on its limited resources. Often unrecognised is that these two issues are linked. The sustainability of a publicly funded NHS (and social care) might require more resources to be allocated to it, but it also requires us to do better with the resources we have. The latter becomes even more important when the options with respect to the former are limited: as they are currently, and seem to be no matter the colour of government going forward. So, let us dismantle the placebos before moving on to a more-positive stance on how we might manage scarcity, including some case studies of how this has worked, in the interest of sustaining our publicly funded systems.

## The Gimmicks and Placebos for Managing Scarcity?

The most common form of managing scarcity in publicly funded health care systems is that of scarcity denial. This commonly manifests itself in the shape of 'reform' or some other management school framework, such as the balanced scorecard, brought in from private industry that occupy management time without consideration of the different context of fixed public sector funding envelopes and hence the need to manage scarcity. Slightly better are attempts at managing scarcity involving squeezing more and more out of the system—often referred to as 'efficiency savings' or, more positively, 'lean thinking'—and the creation of national health technology assessment agencies to assess evidence on the health gains and costs of (often) new pharmaceuticals and procedures to make recommendations as to whether said interventions should be covered by the public purse.

### *Reform*

There used to be a saying that, if you stick a pin in a map and go the nearest government health department, there will be a committee somewhere in the building discussing some aspect of health care reform! However well-intentioned, it could be argued that all that such reforms do is to create new entities within the system which still have to deal with the fact that claims on their resources will be greater than what they have available. Yet, rarely, if ever, is guidance issued on how to do this, an exception being an Advice Note, based on some of the principles expounded in this chapter, issued in support of newly integrated Health and Social Care Partnerships in Scotland in 2016 [2].

The theory of health and social care integration is that, without previously existing financial barriers between health and social care, it becomes easier to move resources around the (now 'integrated') system and address issues such as relieving hospitals of delayed discharges. With people no longer inappropriately placed in hospital, bed space is also freed up to address other unmet needs. But, at least in Scotland, it has not worked out like that [3]. This is due in part to incentives (emanating from how social care is funded—see Chapter 3) to retain people in hospitals, but also challenges in newly created integrated authorities in acting on guidance referred to above to consider what a better balance of care might look like and, thus, move resources from one part of the system to the other.

Table 4.1 contains what I have referred to as platitudes of health care reform. As an economist, they should be music to my ears. But without an accompanying process for how to decide on the right balance of care or how to make decisions based on evidence, platitudes are what these statements remain. There may be some evidence to back up other reforms—again, see Chapters 3 and 5 for coverage of this. The point, here, though, is that whatever new entities are created, they will still have to manage scarcity. But, the reforms themselves, and the disruption cause by their implementation, detract from this reality. Unfortunately, once again, in the UK, we are headed down a reform path. Watch out for the use of similar phrases to those in Table 4.1 and check whether any are accompanied by any guidance on how to enact them.

**Table 4.1** Platitudes of health care reform

| |
|---|
| "We are going to adopt a 'balance of care' model" |
| "It's about effectiveness and efficiency" |
| "We are going to focus on outcomes and take an evidence-based approach" |
| "We are going to involve front-line staff" |
| "We are going to examine how we are using resources and how can we use them differently" |
| Question |
| **"Have we decided on a process for doing all of these?"** |

### *Balanced Scorecard*

The balanced scorecard grew in popularity throughout the public sector, and especially within the UK NHS, in the 1990s and 2000s. An example of such a scorecard, developed for use in health and social care, is provided in Fig. 4.1 [4].

These scorecards were developed from work conducted with several corporate entities by Kaplan and Norton [5]. However, there is very little evidence as to their effectiveness [6]. Although such scorecards take different forms, the basics are as outlined in Fig. 4.1 with consideration given to how each of the surrounding elements contribute to allowing the organisation meet its strategic goals. Despite consideration of costs and value for money, the card does not explicitly recognise that choosing to put more of an organisation's resources into one action may then require those resources to come from elsewhere, especially in a situation of fixed

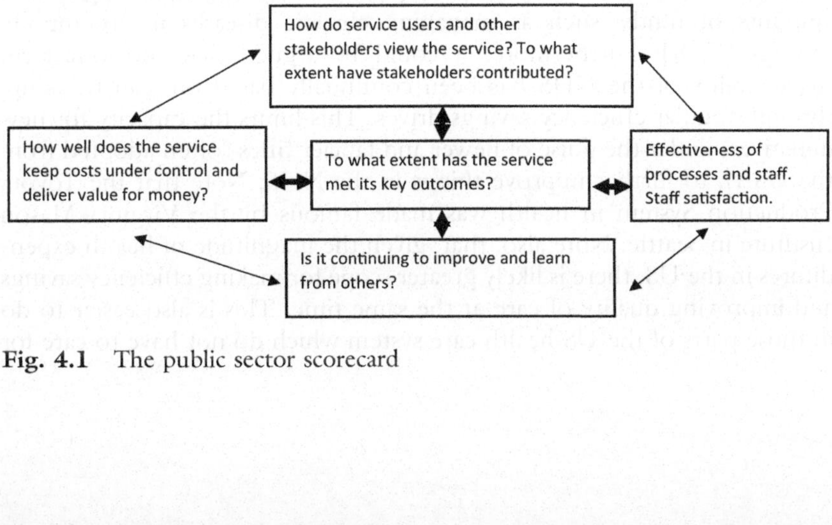


**Fig. 4.1** The public sector scorecard

public sector budgets which may vary only very slightly from year to year. This is different to corporate organisations which are often seeking to grow and, thus, attract more and more of society's resources (or money) in their direction. However, such a framework, in helping organisations focus on how well they are meeting their goals, could be complementary to a process of the sort mapped out further on in this chapter that explicitly recognises scarcity and, thus, that acting to address one goal may have resource consequences that need to be weighed up against competing uses of such resources.

### *Leaning in and Quality of Care*

Who could argue with being treated by the right person in the right place at the right time? Essentially, this is the basis of applying the famous Toyota Production System, reviewing care processes aimed at maintaining (or even improving) quality whilst eliminating waste, often through standard working, to health and social care. Similarly titled initiatives that readers may recognise are 'best value' and, of course, the rounds of 'efficiency savings' that systems commonly embark upon.

It is hard to argue with trying to identify pain-free money; that is, releasing resources in ways that do no harm to existing patients or clients and, hopefully, then allowing such savings to be spent addressing currently unmet needs. However, what is less clear is the extent to which drives towards lean thinking and quality improvement can achieve the magnitudes of savings required to help sustain health and social care systems going forward, either in terms of system affordability or in freeing up resources to switch towards new initiatives which require significant amounts of funds, such as managing chronic diseases in community settings [7, 8]. Furthermore, it could be argued that the long-term sustainability of the NHS has been continually based on lean thinking, through regular efficiency savings drives. This limits the capacity for new initiatives, under the guise of newer and fancier titles (often adopted from the USA), to further improve things in the NHS. Note that the Toyota Production System in health was made famous by the Virginia Mason Institute in Seattle. Note also, that, given the magnitude of health expenditures in the US, there is likely greater scope for making efficiency savings and improving quality of care at the same time. This is also easier to do in those parts of the US health care system which do not have to care for whole-populations as is the case with publicly funded systems such as the NHS.

As a health economist who has worked with many health organisations worldwide in applying priority setting frameworks, of the sort we are about to outline below, I can also testify to such organisations, as the first step in their deliberations about release of resources, resorting to pain-free money as the first port of call. However, if it is not going to deliver all of what is needed in terms of freeing up resources, a broader framework is required. We will get to that after consideration of our final placebo.

### *HTA Agencies*

Rather perversely, I am not a fan of the other global pandemic; that of the creation of health technology assessment (HTA) agencies in many jurisdictions around the world; of which the Pharmaceutical Benefits Advisory Committee (PBAC) in Australia and England's National Institute for Health and Care Excellence (NICE) are pioneering exemplars. To be clear, it is not HTA or HTA agencies that I am against. It is important to have higher-level agencies assessing the evidence on the cost and benefits of new and existing health technologies, including public health and social care. Furthermore, through the publicity emanating from some of their recommendations, these agencies engender important debates in society about what matters when setting priorities in our health and care systems.

The concern is the extent to which such agencies are used as a smokescreen, presenting the façade of managing scarcity whilst never dealing with the trade-offs implied by their recommendations. Often, such agencies assess a new technology, relative to current practice in terms of the additional cost of any gain in health achieved—usually expressed as the incremental cost per quality adjusted life year (or QALY) gained. The higher the incremental cost per QALY gained, the less likely is the new technology to be favoured.

This is all entirely reasonable. However, what such agencies, or the systems within which they operate, fail to recognise is that, even interventions with a low incremental cost per QALY will still require extra resources to be funded at the local level. This is because costs are *incremental* to what is currently happening. At that (local) level of the system, there will be many competing claims on resources. Agencies, such as NICE, therefore, cover only a small fraction of health and care spending in their deliberations. Also, those other competing claims may offer better value for money than actions being recommended—and, remember, in some jurisdictions, like England, health authorities and providers are compelled to act on such advice—simply because they happen to have been assessed by an HTA agency. (In other countries, such as Canada, recommendations are not mandated.)

To reiterate, such agencies need to exist, but the management of scarcity needs to permeate much further into the planning and commissioning processes elsewhere in health and social care systems. But what might that look like?

## Managing Scarcity: The Basic Economic Principles

At any point in time, health and social care entities will be faced with a given mix of resources. Although the nature of claims on such resources are changing all the time, a constant feature is that such claims will be greater than the total resource available. This requires us to think about changing the given mix of resources to better meet the needs, or claims, with which we are faced. Choice is inevitable—this is 'managing scarcity'.

To help manage scarcity, two key economic concepts can be brought to bear. The first is 'opportunity cost' which represents the benefit forgone in the next best alternative use of any given pot of resources. The implication of opportunity cost is that we need to be able to measure the resource inputs (or costs, as well as any cost savings) and benefits (e.g. well-being) associated with alternative claims on resources. This information allows to spend our budget in the best way possible; maximising well-being and, conversely, minimising well-being forgone. But, with such measurement being hard to achieve for everything, this brings us to second economic principle, that of the margin, or marginal analysis. The margin is concerned with change, which is almost always the focus of policy and planning. Questions of resource allocation will normally involve addressing such issues, i.e., should we *expand* services for older people? Should there be *fewer* hospital places for people with mental illness? Should the number of hysterectomies be *increased/decreased*? These are all *questions of change*, leading us to think about marginal costs and marginal benefits. It is comparison of these (cost and benefits at the margin) that can lead us to decide on which changes in services should be implemented.

## Operationalising the Management of Scarcity

Please note that word 'margin' should not be equated with small. Changes examined can be large or small. The notions of opportunity cost and the margin are often operationalised through asking five questions about resource use as listed in Table 4.2.

The first two steps are commonly known as programme budgeting and are based on the logic of 'how can we know what to change if we do not know where we are currently?' Questions 3–5 are the basis of marginal analysis. Note that Question 4 looks very similar to notions of lean thinking discussed above. In economics, we refer to questions addressed under 4 as issues of technical efficiency. Question 5 involves consideration of taking resources from areas of care that, despite being effective, are only so to such a small degree (relative to another option) that some other use of the resources otherwise taken up would be more beneficial. These involve considerations of allocative efficiency, which are more difficult because they involve taking resource from one group of people to give to another; so we can see why, on one hand, resorting to possibilities of pain-free money first, in stage 4, is more preferable, whilst on the other hand, the possibility of going further, if maxed out in technical efficiency terms, is still provided by a more comprehensive framework.

The logic of programme budgeting and marginal analysis (PBMA), a framework used across countries over the last thirty (or more) years, can be applied at any level of the health and social care system where resource scarcity exists and choices have to be made. This may be across a whole health and care system (often referred to as 'macro PBMA') or

**Table 4.2** The five questions about resource use

| | |
|---|---|
| 1. | What resources do we have available in total? |
| 2. | How are those resources currently used? |
| 3. | What would we like to do more of and what would be the implications of these in terms of resources required and improved outcomes? |
| 4. | Are there areas of care which can be provided to the same level of outcome but with less resources? |
| 5. | If not, are there areas of care which, despite being effective, provide less outcomes than some items on our 'wish list' in 3? |

within a programme (often defined by disease [e.g. diabetes] or demography [services for frail older people]). Any particular project can be managed according to standard (but PBMA-adapted) project management processes as in Table 4.3 [9]. Books have been written on how to work through the five questions above and to project manage PBMA [10].

This is a framework that, by 2000, had been used in over 70 health organisations worldwide, with use sustained in many [11]. Our estimates are that this figure is now over 200. The best example in the context rational disinvestment in a situation of financial downturn is that of the Calgary Health Region (CHR) in Canada [12, 13]. Faced with a CA$42 m deficit in 2002–2003, the Provincial Government of Alberta refused to bail CHR out. Instead of an across-the-board cut, a process of rational disinvestment was embarked upon, taking resources from areas of least value. Indeed, 'cuts' of greater than $42 m were realised which then allowed for some new programmes to be invested in. The process has since been replicated in further planning rounds in CHR and also in other Canadian provinces [14].

**Table 4.3** Project managing PBMA

| | |
|---|---|
| (1) | Establish the organisational **objectives** |
| (2) | Ensure there is organisational '**readiness**' |
| (3) | Establish an appropriate **advisory panel** structure |
| (4) | Ensure that **implementation** of results is feasible |
| (5) | Define the **study question** |
| (6) | Choose the most appropriate **programme structure** |
| (7) | Choose an appropriate level of detail for a **programme budget** |
| (8) | Use appropriate methods to **identify options** for investment and disinvestment |
| (9) | **Identify, measure, and value** costs and benefits of investments and disinvestments |
| (10) | Ensure that resource reallocation recommendations are **valid and robust** |

## PBMA in the Modern Age: A Route Out of the Stalemate of Budget-Neutrality

Many reviews of service areas get stuck around Question 3 of our five questions in Table 4.2. That is, review teams know what they want to do more of in order to address unmet needs, but are unable to implement change because they do not think they have the resources, or, amongst some, the ability or capacity to make changes by comparing options. Disillusion often sets in. But, if we can address technical efficiency (Question 4) and even allocative efficiency (Question 5), we then have the freedom to consider how all resources are currently used and whether some things should be given up in order to do more of others.

So, we now have a way forward out of the perceived stalemate of not being able to do anything without extra money. It is also important to note that costs and resources are often thought about in monetary terms. But money is hard to free up in health care systems. If we become more efficient, it just allows the system to do more, rather than always relying on having to take actual money out of one part of the system and plug it in elsewhere. This was illustrated recently in thinking about our biggest resource in health and social care; staff. The key from PBMA thinking is not how much our staff cost (in monetary terms) but, rather, to ensure that our workforce is working to deliver the right clinical outcomes. Thus, PBMA thinking can be brought to bear on big questions such as those in Box 4.1 [15].

Of course, resolution of such issues would require decisions about relative workforce to be made over time in order to achieve a better 'balance of care' model; a model of integrated care more suitable to addressing a key modern issue of managing chronic diseases closer to home. One such model was recently outlined for Scotland [16]. Nevertheless to facilitate such a model, it should be possible to move some staff around the system or cease recruitment of some to employ more of others. At least, that's what the theory of integrated care tells us.

Thinking about recent proposals to reform the NHS and social care, and move towards a model where chronic disease is managed more and more in community settings, the use of PBMA would also help us to understand where the specialist model fails. Taking the maxim of 'which bed did you sleep in last night?' as a guide to where we might want to get to, we can see which communities are delivering quality integrated care and which are not, especially in the over 75 age group. This group represents our largest area of spending in health and social care, many of whom will be in the last year of their life. Previously collected data, referred to as (Multi Agency Inspection of Services for Older People—MAISOP) clearly identified variations in practice throughout Scotland. Continuing this work in in Perth & Kinross, using linked data, we identified that using which-bed-did-you-sleep-in-last-night on a defined locality basis (for this purpose, GP clusters) highlighted important variations in patterns of clinical care [15]. There were no clinical reasons for this, such patterns often representing historic use of existing buildings.

Which-bed-did-you-sleep-in is really a form of PBMA (without the money) as it is really about trying to identify the best 'balance of care'. The best outcomes are where there is high-quality integrated community care—see Box 4.2 for what this means in terms of balance of care.

**Box 4.1 PBMA Without Money: Questions of Staffing**

- In the complicated area of Integrated Community Care, might more home carers or social workers produce better clinical care and outcomes than, say, Accident & Emergency consultants or nurses looking after delayed discharges in a secondary care setting, especially when we know that, despite expanded numbers of such consultants, no improvements in the 4-hour target have been observed (which, it could be argued is problematic in and of itself)?
- Do we need Geriatricians to look after these delayed discharge patients or will we deliver better clinical care if we have more general practitioners?

In the latter case, most of these patients should be being looked after by the extended primary care team. Variations across Scotland show this. We know that general practitioners look after over 60% of the occupied bed days for over-75s' medical admissions in their Community Hospitals in Aberdeenshire; yet in Glasgow they are all under consultant care, mainly geriatricians. The data especially MAISOP (Multi agency inspection of services for older people) all support the view that the Aberdeenshire clinical care produces better outcomes than the Glasgow Model. This is just one of several examples of achieving equivalent (or improved) outcomes alongside potential resource savings which could be put towards meeting currently unmet needs.

Such questions extend beyond delayed discharges and care of older people. For example, publicly available data in Scotland allow us to ask:

- If, in one hospital in Scotland, four orthopaedic surgeons were undertaking 1600 hip replacements per annum in 2006, why now are 20 orthopaedic surgeons in the same hospital delivering a similar number per annum?
- Why are obstetricians in some locations required to look after low-risk pregnancies and is this associated with unwarranted rates of caesarean section deliveries in those same locations?

**Box 4.2 PBMA Without Money: Where Did You Sleep Last Night?**
In the best localities (using the previously collected MAISOP data):

<u>Level 1</u>: at home (own house) no care package. This is at 94% in best areas. 'Length of stay' as long as needed, but under regular review. This just reinforces the important message illustrating what a great success our health and social care can be (Worst is around 90%).
<u>Level 2</u>: at home (own house) with complex care package. 3% in best areas. Length of stay as long as needed, but under regular review (Worst is probably 2%).
<u>Level 3</u>: in nursing/residential home with complex care package. 1% (in best areas). Length of stay should average out to about 1 year (Worst can be up to 3%).
<u>Level 4</u>: in community hospital type bed (hospice, intermediate care, and step down. Delayed discharges-all non-consultant specialist beds. Best is around 1%. Length of stay should average out to about 14–21 days (Worst is 0%).
<u>Level 5</u>: in consultant specialist bed with agreement of GP and Consultant = less than 1%-length of stay should average out to about 7 days (Worst is up to 3%).

The poorest are where there are high numbers of delayed discharges or people spending longer than needed in nursing homes. We know 2% of patients take up 79% of occupied bed days (OBDs) and that we have around 1600 OBDs due to delayed discharges. That is equivalent to filling two District General Hospitals (out of roughly 20 in Scotland) with patients who will be better looked after in a community setting. Using PBMA thinking, each community could look at where they are now with respect to 'which bed you slept in last night?' and what this means for resource spending, and, from that, map out a better balance of care and plan for how to get there. To an extent, this would allow us to move away from finance and austerity as the excuses for avoiding change to how best to train and retain staff doing the right job in the right place with the right patients. It may seem simplistic, but thinking about resource re-allocations to bring people closer to home brings into play £1 billion currently spent on unproductive delayed discharges [3]. Returning to the issue of sustainability, if we can do this, then we minimise the most difficult choices, reducing opportunity costs, so maintaining belief in and support for publicly funded systems.

### *A Framework Created by Integrated Care Managers*

All the way through this chapter, the idea of a process has been promoted without ever having revealed one. Recently, in working with managers in health and social care integration bodies in Scotland, we have produced such a framework [17]. The interesting thing about this framework, replicated in Fig. 4.2, is that it was produced, not by the authors alone, but in a co-productive exercise with those managers in which they were given a blank page and asked to outline a process for how, in a budget-neutral situation, they would get from 'current allocation of resources' to 'recommendations for change'. Further reasons for leaving presentation of this framework until the end of the chapter are that it emphasises three further important points: one of which is the need to set, and assess options against, explicit priority setting criteria, which almost always include, amongst others, gains in health or well-being and some notion of equity in access; the second being that the exercise resulted not only in an economics-based process, but that process is strongly related to ideas from multi-criteria decision-making and is underpinned by notions of ethics from Accountability for Reasonableness, all in one framework which is itself 'integrated' [18, 19]; and, finally, to show that this work continues and to leave readers with a framework they might like to try to follow in their own resource-constrained environments.

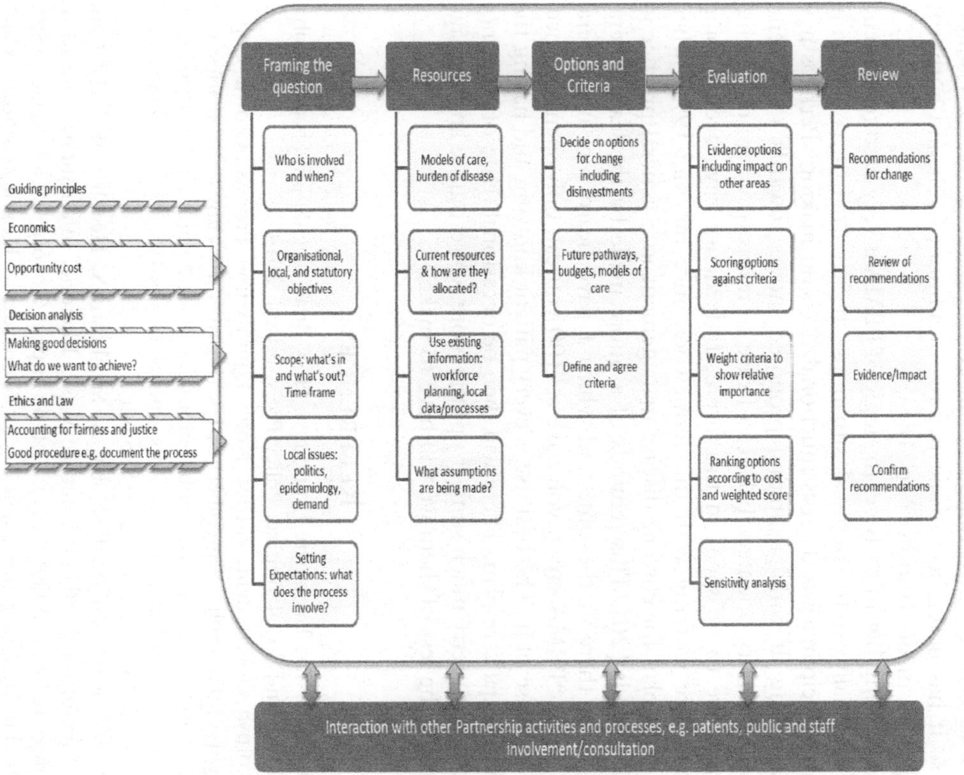


**Fig. 4.2** An economics and ethics-based framework for priority setting

## Conclusion

Maybe PBMA's time has come. It does, however, follow advice of Bevan in *In Place of Fear* in 1952 to "not allow ourselves to be deterred from the effort to introduce rational principles into social relations simply because it has never been done before – tradition, habit and authority having been made to suffice" (p. 181).

In following Bevan's advice, the logic of PBMA is very hard to contend with, especially in tough fiscal situations. It is participatory, allowing for inter-disciplinary and cross-functional decision-making. Perhaps it is now a strong fit with facilitating proposed moves towards a different, more community-oriented, balance of care in terms of where our caring resources are to be spent in the future. Indeed, we have been hoping for this since working with this framework since the mid-1990s when using it to plan for chronic disease management in a general practice in the Highlands [20]. This reminds of a quote made by the lead general practitioner there at the time and which I have heard him use several times since: "PBMA says if you have a £100 you can only spend it once. Make best use of it. The best use is every patient knowing and having the best individual care plan. There will then be occasional trade-offs but not many." That pretty much sums it up; the more we recognise and manage trade-offs, the less of them we will have to make!

## References

1. Sheard S. The Passionate Economist: How Brian Abel-Smith Shaped Global Health and Social Welfare. Policy Press, Bristol, 2014.
2. Scottish Government. Advice Note: Prioritisation Process. Crown Copyright, Edinburgh, September 2016 (https://www.gov.scot/binaries/content/documents/govscot/publications/advice-and-guidance/2016/09/advice-note-prioritisation-process/documents/00505886-pdf/00505886-pdf/govscot%3Adocument/00505886.pdf).
3. Donaldson C, Knight P, Noble A, Strathearn S. Health and Social Care Integration in Scotland: Evidence Versus Rhetoric. International Journal of Integrated Care 2024; 24 (1): 4, 1–4 (https://doi.org/10.5334/ijic.7759).
4. Moulin M. Using the Public Sector Scorecard in Health and Social Care. In Neely A, Kennerley M and Walters A (eds) Performance Measurement and Management: Public ad Private. Papers form the Fourth International Conference of the Performance Measurement Association, PMA, Centre for Business Performance, Cranfield School of Management, 2004.

5. Kaplan RS and Norton DP. The Balanced Scorecard: Measures That Drive Performance. Harvard Business Review 1992; 70: 71–79.
6. Neely A, Kennerley M and Martinet V. Does the Balanced Scorecard Work? An Empirical Investigation. In Neely A, Kennerley M and Walters A (eds) Performance Measurement and Management: Public ad Private. Papers form the Fourth International Conference of the Performance Measurement Association, PMA, Centre for Business Performance, Cranfield School of Management, 2004.
7. Ovretveit J. Does Improving Quality Save Money? Health Foundation, London, 2009.
8. Woodnutt S. Is Lean Systaiunable in Today's NHS Hospitals? A Systematic Literature Review Using the Meta-Narrative and Integrative Methods. International Journal for Quality in Health Care 2018; 30: 578–586.
9. Peacock S, Ruta D, Mitton C, Donaldson C, Bate A and Murtagh M. Using Economics for Pragmatic and Ethical Priority Setting: Two Checklists for Doctors and Managers. British Medical Journal 2006; 332: 482–485.
10. Mitton C, Donaldson C. Priority Setting Toolkit: A Practical Guide to the Use of Economics in Health Care Decision Making. BMJ Books, London, 2004.
11. Mitton C and Donaldson C. 25 Years of Programme Budgeting and Marginal Analysis in the Health Sector. Journal of Health Services Research and Policy 2001; 6: 239–248.
12. Mitton C, Patten S, Waldner H and Donaldson C. Priority Setting in Health Authorities: A Novel Approach to a Historical Activity. Social Science and Medicine 2003; 57: 1653–1663.
13. Patten S, Mitton C and Donaldson C. Using Participatory Action Research to Build a Priority Setting Process in a Canadian Regional Health Authority. Social Science and Medicine 2006; 63: 1121–1134.
14. Donaldson C, Bate A, Mitton C, Dionne F and Ruta D. Rational Disinvestment. Quarterly Journal of Medicine 2010; 103:801–807.
15. Donaldson C and Noble A. Gain with Least Pain: Using Economics Thinking to Advance Population Health in a Budget-Neutral World. Reform Scotland series on NHS 2048, 5th May 2024.
16. Marr G. Through Recovery to Reform. Reform Scotland (www.reformscotland.com), 10th April 2024.
17. Collins M, Baker R, Morton A, Syrett K, Frith L, Donaldson C. Developing a Combined Framework for Priority Setting in Integrated Health and Social Care Settings. BMC Health Services Research 2023; 23: 879. https://doi.org/10.1186/s12913-023-09866-x.
18. Peacock SJ et al. Priority Setting in Health Care Using Multi-attribute Utility Theory and Programme Budgeting and Marginal Analysis. Social Science and Medicine 2007; 64: 897.

19. Gibson JL, Mitton C, Martin DK, Donaldson C, Singer PA. Ethics and Economics: Does Program Budgeting and Marginal Analysis Contribute to Fair Priority Setting? Journal of Health Services Research & Policy 2006; 11(1): 32–37.
20. Scott A, Currie S, Donaldson C. Evaluating Innovation in General Practice: A Pragmatic Framework Using Programme Budgeting and Marginal Analysis. Family Practice 1998; 15:216–222.

CHAPTER 5

# What Do We Do About Doctors? Countervailing Power (In)Action

**Abstract** There are two aspects to the economics of the medical profession. The first is that of how we should pay them and, of course, how much. From research, there are tried and tested lessons that essentially lead us to a system of remuneration, especially for doctors as the main controllers of resource use in the system, that is based on 'horses for courses'; a mixed system of remuneration across salaries, fees-per-item-of-service, capitation and others. Despite what some, including health economists, might say, no one of these forms of remuneration is completely wrong or completely right. The particular mix in any given context should be based on what funders (usually governments) are trying to achieve. Secondly, we need to decide on how many of each category of staff we need. Previous ways of planning have obviously not worked, but we keep returning to the same well, reinforcing vested interests, and arriving at periodic staffing crises of which the current one is one of the worst and seemingly (but only seemingly) intractable. There are straightforward ways of doing this better that have only rarely been implemented. These better account for potential to measure real needs and thus match the numbers and types of professionals required to address them. This includes accounting for the potential to substitute advanced nurse practitioners and allied health professionals in roles traditionally seen as the preserve of the medical profession.

© The Author(s), under exclusive license to Springer Nature Switzerland AG 2025

C. Donaldson, *Financing Health and Social Care*,
https://doi.org/10.1007/978-3-031-86769-9_5

**Keywords** Incentives · Fee-for-service · Workforce planning · Skill mix · Substitution

*Health economists often take great glee in catching doctors 'at it'. This is embodied in the more-formal notion of supplier-induced demand; the power of doctors to recommend service provision beyond what a fully informed consumer would demand. Often, however, there are alternative explanations. If more doctors are made available, then access costs are reduced and, thus, more services are provided—a standard 'market forces' response. Or, if we pay doctors in particular ways and in particular amounts for particular services, they will respond by providing more (or less) of them. The important thing is that this provides an important tool for health policy. Along with a lack of proper planning for how many doctors we might want in the first place, many governments have not harnessed this potential.*

Readers might recall that, in Chapter 2, we introduced the requirement for countervailing power on the part of government to combat the power of the medical profession. This power is granted to medicine via the (correct) granting of licensure in order to maintain standards in the delivery of care due, in large part, to a lack of knowledge on the part of consumers as to what works best. In these senses there is no conventional separation of supply and demand in the way that we can portray for other commodities. The consequences of this are not only the need for significant government intervention in the funding of health and social care but also the use of the countervailing power of government to plan the system. This involves negotiating with powerful bodies, such as the medical profession with respect to how they are remunerated—because, as will be seen, we know that doctors—just like most people—respond to financial incentives—and also how many doctors we need in total and relative to other professional groups. How to pay doctors and how many of them to have (alongside numbers of other health professions) deals with two of three 'how' questions with respect to workforce, articulated by Robert Elliott as the key policy questions for workforce planning in his comprehensive text on *The Economics of the UK Health and Social Care Labour Market* [1]. The other question is how much to pay them, which we will leave for Chapter 7. Before proceeding, it is also worth busting one more myth, which is the oft-repeated claim that the NHS labour force is unproductive. First, Elliott argues that, due to health and social care being predominantly a personal service industry, technology will not displace labour in the same way it has in other sectors of the economy, and that high-quality, empathetic, patient-centred care is critical to the quality of health outcomes [1]. Secondly, he also shows, via use of English hospital output data (such as finished consultant episodes and outpatient attendances) relative to input growth, that the growth in productivity in health and social care between 2010 and 2020 was around double the rate for the whole economy [1].

Although some of the arguments presented here apply to other health professionals, the reason that doctors are key is because they are the main resource users in any system. Many costs are the result of their direct clinical decisions or their decisions, via referrals, to move people (patients and clients) around the system. So, how we pay doctors and how many of them we have are crucial to system efficiency and equity. On the former, beyond occasional disputes over rates of pay, it is fair to say that, in many jurisdictions, including the UK, we have the blend of remuneration about right. Although, as will be illustrated, this is not always the case across the globe, this shows that countervailing power *in* action can work. However, there is also a significant degree of countervailing power *inaction* on the part of governments that leaves the medical profession with too much influence over how they are paid and, in terms of workforce planning, on entry to the profession and the abilities of others, such as nurse practitioners, to take on more of the load.

Hence the ambiguous title of this chapter. It is these issues of remuneration and workforce planning that we want to work through here, the good news being that there is plenty of health economics research to inform a better way forward for each.

## Paying Doctors

Earlier, in Chapter 3, when introducing ideas such as internal markets, we were essentially discussing the idea of financial incentives for health care institutions, such as hospitals. One other way in which financial incentives in health care have been popularised, and shown to work, is in influencing the behaviour of individuals as opposed to such institutions. With doctors making most of the resource-committing decisions in health care, they have inevitably become the most studied health profession in this regard. Also, most other health professions are remunerated via a salaried system.

Doctors, on the other hand experience different forms of remuneration which then influence these decisions.

For example, the most common form of remuneration globally is that of fee-for-service (FFS). In crude terms, a primary care physician might be paid a fee for each consultation undertaken or a surgeon may command a fee for each operation conducted. FFS can also be refined and targeted at specific items of care. For hospital doctors, the main alternative to FFS would be a salary. Such salaries can be graded for status through, for example, a system of merit awards of the sort that exists in the UK and which, at the highest levels, can double the salary of a hospital consultant. Hospital doctors may also be free to spend (usually limited) time working for private payment. For primary care doctors, the main alternative to FFS is that of capitation whereby, for each person registered with a primary care doctor, the doctor receives a fixed annual pre-payment. Also, it does not have to be one or the other. Capitation might be used to encourage more preventive activities whilst FFS could also be added in order to encourage high rates of provision of particular services, such as immunisations, vaccinations or cervical smears. Such mixed forms of remuneration tend to be known as 'blended payment' systems.

All of this is important because these different forms of remuneration will lead to different behaviours on the part of doctors. It has long been known that rates of surgery are higher in hospital-based systems relying on FFS and that, with a target income in mind, doctors will provide more services in response to increased doctor-to-population ratios in defined geographic areas [2, 3]. A famous study, too, has shown that it is possible to encourage switching of services from higher-cost environments, such as hospitals, into primary care by offering fees to general practitioners for providing particular items of diagnostic and curative service [4].

A more recent example is that of the UK NHS, which, in 2004, implemented a Quality and Outcomes Framework (QoF) accounting for around 25% of the income of family practitioners. The scheme has been subjected to various changes and discussions of its relative merits over time. However, an opportunity to provide some evidence on the QoF was presented by removal of some 40 of the 121 financial incentives in March 2014 (end of fiscal year 2013–2014) [5]. The study compared experiences for 12 of the indicators for which incentives were removed, compared with 6 for which the incentives were maintained. The data used documented clinical processes and intermediate outcomes for each of three years before and three years after removal of the incentives. (Data on those incentives which were removed continued to be collected.) Details of all 18 of these indicators are provided in Table 5.1, with results presented in Table 5.2.

Most striking are the large drops in documented service provision for areas of care from which the QoF incentive was withdrawn. The largest reductions were for provision of advice. Smaller reductions occurred for areas of important clinical process. Of course, these changes could be due to lower levels of provision or of documentation, although that would beg the question as to why reductions are not similar across the board, the authors concluding that reductions in quality were likely.

Some health economists would interpret these results as evidence of supplier-induced demand, demonstrating doctors' abilities to switch their attention to areas of care which are, perhaps, more financially rewarding and can be used to maintain their 'target income'. Less controversially, we can say that doctors are human after all. They respond to incentives. The key, then, is to decide on objectives and then keep a range of remuneration options open to ensure that the objectives are met. For some of the QoF items documented above, it may be that it is judged better (i.e. a more efficient use of resources) for their provision to be reduced. If that is the case, an important lesson is that it is possible to combine lessons from evidence-based medicine as to what is more efficient with financial incentives to encourage its provision (as well as to discourage whatever is deemed less efficient).

There are examples, too, where changing incentives can go wrong, a well-known case being introduction of capitation to replace FFS in Health Services Organisations (HSOs) in Ontario in the 1970s. Contrary to expectations, capitation did not reduce hospitalisations in capitation-remunerated practices when compared with a control group of general practitioners who remained in the dominant FFS system [6]. A number of explanations for this are put forward in an excellent paper on the historical context of the experiment [7]. The main reason put forward is that the scheme was voluntary and, therefore, the capitation group was populated by practitioners who were already in agreement with the philosophy of such a payment system—they were already low referrers and would, therefore, be unlikely to become even lower referrers as a result of switching to capitation. This was exacerbated by the capitation rates having been calculated according to previous provincial-level average FFS payments. Capitation-based practices, therefore, received payments which were greater than their already low-cost practice style warranted.

**Table 5.1** Quality-of-care indicators included in the analysis*

| *Indicator* | *Indicator type* | *Period with incentives* | *Maximum payment per average-size practice (US dollars)*** | *Median no of patients eligible for care per practice (IQR)**** |
|---|---|---|---|---|
| *Incentives removed* | | | | |
| Smoking status documents in all adults | Clinical process | 2010–2011 to 2013–2014 | £1,726 ($2,313) | 5260 (3293–7992) |
| Diabetes retinopathy screening documented | Clinical process | 2010–2011 to 2013–2014 | £785 ($1,051) | 319 (205–474) |
| Glycated haemoglobin testing documented in patients with serious mental health illness§ | Clinical process | 2011–2012 to 2013–2014 | £785 ($1,051) | 29 (17–46) |
| Body-mass index documented in patients with serious mental health issues | Clinical process | 2011–2012 to 2013–2014 | £628 ($841) | 47 (29–76) |
| Thyroid function tested in patients with hypothyroidism | Clinical process | 2010–2011 to 2013–2014 | £942 ($1.262) | 192 (110–308) |
| Cholesterol tested in patients with stroke or TIA | Clinical process | 2010–2011 to 2013–2014 | £314 ($421) | 98 (51–164) |
| Cholesterol controlled in patients with stroke or TIA | Intermediate outcome | 2010–2011 to 2013–2014 | £785 ($1,051) | 62 (30–109) |
| Cholesterol controlled in patients with CHD | Intermediate Outcome | 2010–2011 to 2013–2014 | £2,668 ($3,575) | 190 (106–306) |
| Patients with epilepsy documented as being seizure-free | Intermediate outcome | 2010–2011 to 2013–2014 | £942 ($1.262) | 36 (21–58) |
| Lifestyle advice documented in patients with hypertension | Health advice | 2010–2011 to 2013–2014 | £1,569 ($2.103) | 178 (111–275) |

(continued)

**Table 5.1** (continued)

| *Indicator* | *Indicator type* | *Period with incentives* | *Maximum payment per average-size practice (US dollars)*** | *Median no of patients eligible for care per practice (IQR)**** |
|---|---|---|---|---|
| Preconception advice documented in patients with epilepsy | Health advice | 2011–2012 to 2013–2014 | £471 ($631) | 9 (5–15) |
| Advice about using long-acting, reversible contraceptives documented | Health advice | 2010–2011 to 2013–2014 | £471 ($631) | 333 (187–553) |
| *Incentives maintained* | | | | |
| Blood pressure documented in patients with serious mental illness§ | Clinical process | 2011–2012 to 2016–2017 | £628 ($841) | 47 (28–74) |
| Alcohol Consumption documented in patients with serious mental illness§ | Clinical process | 2011–2012 to 2016–2017 | £628 ($841) | 47 (28–74) |
| Cholesterol controlled in patients with diabetes | Intermediate outcome | 2010–2011 to 2016–2017 | £942 ($1,262) | 327 (203–492) |
| Blood pressure controlled in patients with CHD | Intermediate outcome | 2010–2011 to 2016–2017 | £2,668 ($3,575) | 206 (116–335) |
| Blood pressure controlled in patients with stroke or TIA | Intermediate outcome | 2010–2011 to 2016–2017 | £785 ($1,051) | 108 (55–179) |
| Smoking-cessation advice documented in smokers with chronic conditions◆ | Health advice | 2010–2011 to 2016–2017 | £3,923 ($5,527) | 223 (138–349) |

*CHD denotes coronary heart disease, IQR interquartile range, and TIA transient ischemic attack

**Table 5.2** Changes in documented quality of care according to whether incentives were removed or maintained

| *Indicator* | *Patients Receiving Indicated Care before Incentive Removal* % of patients (95% CI)* | *Absolute Change in Expected Trend after Incentive Removal 1 year post-removal 3 year post-removal Percentage points (95% CI)* | |
|---|---|---|---|
| *Incentives removed* | | | |
| Smoking status documents in all adults | 85.5 (85.5–85.5) | –5.8 (–8.9 to –2.7) | –11.7 (–16.3 to 7.1) |
| Diabetes retinopathy screening documented | 82.6 (82.5–82.6) | –11.5 (–16.7 to 6.3) | –14.9 (–22.7 to –7.1) |
| Glycated haemoglobin testing documented in patients with serious mental health illness | 75.8 (75.5–76.1) | –28.5 (–39.0 to 18.0) | –37.5 (–55.4 to –19.6) |
| Body-mass index documented in patients with serious mental health issues | 80.1 (79.9–80.3) | –30.2 (–35.5 to –24.9) | –29.9 (–38.9 to 20.9) |
| Thyroid function tested in patients with hypothyroidism | 93.5 (93.5–93.6) | –12.1 (–13.6 to –10.6) | –9.2 (–11.4 to –7.0) |
| Cholesterol tested in patients with stroke or TIA | 85.2 (85.1–85.3) | –19.8 (–22.4 to –17.2) | –18.0 (–21.8 to –14.2) |
| Cholesterol controlled in patients with stroke or TIA | 69.1 (68.9–69.3) | –15.9 (–17.1 to –14.7) | –16.8 (–18.0 to –15.0) |
| Cholesterol controlled in patients with CHD | 74.1 (74.0–74.2) | –10.7 (–13.6 to –7.8) | –10.1 (–14.3 to –5.9) |
| Patients with epilepsy documented as being seizure-free | 61.7 (61.4–62.0) | –48.7 (–51.8 to –45.6) | –53.6 (–58.2 to –49.0) |

(continued)

**Table 5.2** (continued)

| *Indicator* | *Patients Receiving Indicated Care before Incentive Removal* % of patients (95% CI)* | *Absolute Change in Expected Trend after Incentive Removal 1 year post-removal 3 year post-removal Percentage points (95% CI)* | |
|---|---|---|---|
| Lifestyle advice documented in patients with hypertension | 80.1 (80.0–80.2) | –62.3 (–65.6 to –59.0) | –71.6 (–76.5 to –66.7) |
| Preconception advice documented in patients with epilepsy | 64.9 (64.3–65.4) | –60.5 (–63.5 to –57.5) | –65.9 (–71.0 to -60.8)** |
| Advice about using long-acting, reversible contraceptives documented | 88.2 (88.1–88.3) | –36.6 (–39.9 to –33.3) | –46.1 (–51.8 to –45.6) |
| *Incentives maintained**** | | | |
| Blood pressure documented in patients with serious mental illness§ | 83.0 (82.9–83.1) | –1.5 (–5.4 to 2.4) | 0.2 (–6.5 to 6.9) |
| Alcohol Consumption documented in patients with serious mental illness§ | 79.1 (79.0–79.2) | 0.3 (–6.9 to 7.5) | 1.5 (–10.7 to 13.7) |
| Cholesterol controlled in patients with diabetes | 72.3 (72.3–72.4) | –0.4 (–0.8 to 0.05) | 0.0 (–0.7 to 0.7) |
| Blood pressure controlled in patients with CHD | 88.9 (88.8–88.9) | –0.8 (–1.6 to –0.04) | –1.4 (–2.5 to-0.3) |

(continued)

**Table 5.2** (continued)

| *Indicator* | *Patients Receiving Indicated Care before Incentive Removal** % of patients (95% CI)* | *Absolute Change in Expected Trend after Incentive Removal 1 year post-removal 3 year post-removal Percentage points (95% CI)* | |
|---|---|---|---|
| Blood pressure controlled in patients with stroke or TIA | 85.6 (85.6–85.6) | –1.7 (–2.5 to –0.9) | –2.4 (–3.5 to –1.3) |
| Smoking-cessation advice documented in smokers with chronic conditions | 93.2 (93.2–93.2) | 0.6 (0.2 to 1.4) | 0.9 (–0.2 to 2.0) |

*Values are population means for the year before incentive removal

**The estimated reduction is greater than the value in the year before incentive removal because there was a small upward trend in this indicator before incentive removal, so the expected value 3 years after removal was slightly larger

***In the analysis of indicators for which incentives were maintained, we examined whether there was a change in performance after an assumed interruption on the date of incentive removal for other indicators (at the end of 2013–2014)

Assuming that the FFS-based practices just carried on as before, not much changed in overall practice but overall costs rose. This is a great example of how we require good contextual evidence on how not to set up new remuneration schemes, or at least to think through what any unintended consequences might be. But the main lesson is that any such reforms should not be voluntary. If they are, then the new scheme will attract those who can gain financially, whilst those who would lose out will opt to remain in the existing scheme. Costs will rise for no patient or population benefit.

Returning to the UK's QoF reforms in 2004, they could also be portrayed as an example of policy-making gone wrong. The error of policy-makers was in not recognising that general practitioners are very good at responding to incentives and, thus, an underestimation was made as to how well they would do so when offered a set of payments for meeting various quality standards [8]. Consequently, when compared with seven other countries in Northern and Western Europe, by 2005, UK general practitioners rose from being just above the middle of the pack in terms of income to being the best paid, and by some distance [9]. This is reinforced by data showing that, by 2005, doctors had reached the peak of how well they were paid relative to the rest of the UK population. By 2005, they were paid 2.6 times the average of all employees [1]. (This has, however, declined to now being at its worst ever level when compared with all other employees and to other frontline clinical professionals, but more on pay levels in Chapter 7, although evidence is now emerging a crisis of recruitment and, relatedly, threats to sustainabiity of the traditional partnership model and its associated advantages of local accountability and care continuity).

Broadly, it is not wise to remunerate hospital physicians by FFS—yet, some major countries, such as the US and Canada, being dominated by FFS, have some way to go in recognising and repairing this. Bevan predicted this in 1952 in *In Place of Fear*:

> Danger of abuse in the Health Service is always at the point where private commercialism impinges on the Service; where, for example, the optician, is paid for the spectacles he himself prescribes, or the dentist gives an unnecessary filling for which he is paid. (p. 108)

Other countries, like the UK, where hospital doctors receive a salary (along with other bonus-type rewards that are presented as one's career advances) have it broadly right. In primary care it is good to maintain blended systems, with FFS for some activities and capitation for others. Again, countries operating largely FFS-based primary care systems will not be doing well in terms of encouraging prevention and integration with the wider health care system. Other forms of payment might work, too. These could be in the form of target payments, triggering different levels of payment for different rates of coverage achieved, for example in screening. Also, it is useful to keep the option of paying quite high salaries in primary care to encourage doctors to practice in locations to which it is difficult to recruit, or indeed, further upward adjustment of budgets paid to practitioners in such locations. The key is to establish objectives, and evidence with regard to how best to achieve such objectives, before then deciding on the mixed system of financial incentives to meet these objectives. Some countries have more work to do on this than others.

## How Many Doctors (and Other Health Professionals)?

Contradictions abound with respect to planning the health and care workforce. There always seem to be shortages, even when, during the 1990s and 2000s, supply (e.g. number of practising doctors per 1000 population) showed substantial increases in many countries, including the UK [10]. More recently in the UK, there is no doubt that many professions as whole, such as nursing, and particular areas of practice, such as primary care, have stalled in terms of numbers and are also experience difficulties in recruitment to existing vacancies [11]. In some countries, like Canada, this has played out in terms of major access issues over the last decade with large proportions of the population not having ready access to GPs. The one consistency that many countries experience is a lack of sophistication in workforce planning, with periods of relative glut or scarcity that seem to be out of line with population needs. As well as political expediency, models of planning are still based on staff-population ratios, which, despite being able to account for changes in population numbers, are locked into models of current practice and do not account for changes in the health of those populations. What makes this even more strange is that advances have been made in incorporating the notion of 'need' into more-general resource allocation formulae—i.e. the mechanisms that aid decisions about how to divide the total health care budget across different, largely geographical, jurisdictions [12, 13]. This would seem to indicate that other forces, such as the power and protectionism of professions, are at play.

Examining this in more detail, it is reasonable to expect that the prime consideration for planning the size of the health workforce in any country would be that of need. The general approach, and one that applies across many countries, is to increase the total amount of resources allocated on an annual, incremental basis (allocation based on history), adjusted for the ageing of the population and the ever-rising expectations of the public. With respect to the former, current rates of service use, and therefore costs, are applied to future population projections [1], which ignores two key dynamics. First, over time, the same age cohorts, although changing in size, tend to be healthier. So, although rates of service use for those in older age groups might be expected to be higher on average compared with such rates in younger groups, if more people in older age groups are rating their health as 'good', we cannot necessarily apply current rates of service use amongst current groups of older people to future groups of the same age [14]. Second, technological change can enhance the productivity of the resources allocated, and, in many cases, might mean that less medical time is required per procedure carried out, even if more of the procedures themselves might be needed and, indeed, can now be carried out due to being less invasive and applied to older people who are healthier than before. Without accounting for these aspects of epidemiological and technological change over time, workforce planning is in danger of simply reinforcing existing inefficiencies. Such models also show that it is not the ageing of the population per se that is to blame for rising health care costs but rather the fact that we can do more for older people due to technological improvement and their ability to withstand treatment (e.g. less-invasive surgery) that may not have been possible before. This is, generally, a good thing, but it costs money.

Of course, this is all made more complicated by particular labour force characteristics. It takes several years to train health professionals. Preferences for labour force participation (e.g. moves towards more part-time work) and opportunities overseas can be heavily influenced by things like rates of pay. Yet it is unclear whether pay review bodies account for such factors when making recommendations over pay to governments.

With respect to rising expectations it is important to remember our concept of supplier-induced demand whereby such expectations are not independent of advice from health care providers. This advice extends into health policy debates too, with documented evidence of representative groups of medical practitioners recommending things like extending the definitions of their patient groups (e.g. age groups covered by paediatricians), barring other routes to care and finding other things to do to children (hence the rise in orthodontics) [15, 16].

Such protectionism takes us into the realms of potential for substitution of medical labour with that from other allied health professions. It is now well-evidenced that nurse practitioners can undertake many of the clinical tasks which, in the past, would have been seen as the preserve of physicians [17, 18]. The same applies to other labour force innovations, such as use of physician associates and pharmacists. But constraints still abound. Recently, a strong case has been made for expanding the nurse practitioner workforce in Canada [19]. However, this is often implemented in an environment in which physicians, despite seeking to reduce their own inputs, try to retain their income levels, and so more resources overall are required [20]. Only in September of 2024, pharmacists in the

UK voted to work to rule in protest at the amount of NHS work they are being asked to take on without requisite financial compensation [21].

Much of this is still in control of the medical profession in terms of influence over government and ability to employ non-medical staff. We also need to be open to even more radical solutions to labour substitution. For example, I am often intrigued as to why the model of the famous Cuckoo Lane Practice in London is not more widespread [22]. This nurse-led general practice employs a just few hours of medical time each day. It is an innovation that is now spreading to other parts of the UK and could be an important part of solving the crisis in access to primary care.

## Conclusions

Populations are changing and so are their needs. Note the growing numbers of people living in communities with long-term chronic diseases that require management. Models of future workforce planning should be sophisticated enough to account for this. Indeed, there are already examples out there in the literature to demonstrate this [23]. Such models can also account for the changes in skill mix which are also required to enhance quality of care and perhaps even save resources and account for moves towards more integrated health and social care systems [24, 25]. If they can be implemented, they could also facilitate less reliance on temporary staff along with higher rates of pay required to retain people in longer-term employment within health and social care. Earlier chapters, with their examples of integrated care, show that moves to more multi-disciplinary teams that can be better planned for are essential going forward.

Once we have staff in place, we also know that they can be further incentivised through different form of financial remuneration. This is most likely to apply to paying doctors in ways that encourage more efficient delivery of care. Although some experimentation with different levels of payment forms might be required from time to time, governments simply need to decide on the objectives they want to achieve with respect to population health and choose the appropriate blended payment system best placed to achieve it. In many respects, the UK has led the way on this, and the lessons are there for other countries to pick up on. But, for all countries, including the UK, governments need the courage to engage the profession in maximising benefit to the community from better tools for workforce planning and in paying doctors.

## References


1. Elliott R. The Economics of the UK Health and Social Care Labour Market: How Labour Economics Can Inform Policy Towards the Frontline Labour Force. Oxford University Press, Oxford, 2024.
2. Vayda E. A Comparison of Surgical Rates in Canada and in England and Wales. New England Journal of Medicine 1973; 289: 1224-1229.
3. Cromwell J and Mitchell JB. Physician-Induced Demand for Surgery. Journal of Health Economics 1986; 5: 293-313.
4. Krasnik A, Groenewegen PP, Pedersen PA, von Scholten P, Mooney G, Gottschau A, Flierman HA and Damsgaard MT. Changing Remuneration Systems: Effects on Activity in General Practice. British Medical Journal 1990; 300:1698–1701.
5. Minchin M, Roland M, Richardsson J, Rowark S and Guthrie B. Quality of Care in the United Kingdom After Removal of Financial Incentives. New England Journal of Medicine 2018: 379: 948–957.
6. Hutchison B, Birch S, Hurley J, Lomas J and Fawne S-D. Do Physician-Payment Mechanisms Affect Hospital Utilization. A Study of Health Service Organizations in Ontario. Canadian Medical Association Journal 1996; 154: 653–661.
7. Gillick J, Hutchison B and Birch S. Capitation and Primary Care in Canada: Financial Incentives and the Evolution of Health Service Organisations. International Journal of Health Services 2001; 31: 583–603.
8. National Audit Office. NHS Pay Modernisation: New Contract for General Practice Services in England. Report by the Comptroller and Auditor General. HC-307, Session 2007–2008, February 2008.
9. Kroneman MW, Van der See J, Groot W. Income Development of General Practitioners in Eight European Countries from 1975 to 2005. BMC Health Services Research 2009; 9: 26 (https://doi.org/10.1186/1472-6963-9-26).
10. Anderson M, O'Neill C, MacLeod Clark J, Street A, Woods M, Johnston-Webber C, Charlesworth A, White M, Foster M, Majeed A, Pitchforth E, Mossialos E, Asaria M, McGuire A. Securing a Sustainable and Fit-for-Purpose UK Health and Care Workforce. Lancet 2021; 397(10288): 1992–2011 (https://doi.org/10.1016/S0140-6736(21)00231-2. Epub 2021 May 6. PMID: 33965066; PMCID: PMC9634455)
11. Birch S, Mason T, Sutton M and Whittaker W. Not Enough Doctors or Not Enough Needs? Refocusing Health Workforce Planning from Providers and

Services to Populations and Needs. Journal of Health Services Research & Policy 2013; 18(2): 107–113.

12. Eyles J, Birch S, Chambers et al. A Needs-Based Methodology for Allocating Health-Care Resources in Ontario: Development and Application. Social Science & Medicine 1991; 33: 489–500.
13. Gravelle H, Sutton M, Morris S, Windmeijer F, Leyland A, Dibben C, Muirhead M. Modelling Supply and Demand Influences of the Use of Health Care: Implications for Deriving a Needs-Based Capitation Formula. Health Economics 2002; 12: 985–1004.
14. Mason T, Sutton M, Whittaker W and Birch S. Exploring the Limitations of Age-Based Models for Health Care Planning. Social Science & Medicine 2015; 132: 11-19.
15. Pettigrew LM, Petersen I, Mays N, Cromwell D. The changing shape of English general practice: a retrospective longitudinal study using national datasets describing trends in organisational structure, workforce and recorded appointments. BMJ Open 2024; 14: e081535. https://doi.org/10.1136/bmjopen-2023-081535.
16. Shipman S, Lurie J and Goodman D. The General Paediatrician: Projecting Future Workforce Supply and Requirements. Pediatrics 2004; 113: 435-442.
17. Birch S, Tomblin Murphy G, Mackenzie A, Whittaker W and Mason T. Will the Need-Based Planning of Health Human Resources Currently Undertaken in Several Countries Lead to Excess Supply and Inefficiency? A Comment on Basu and Pak. Health Economics 2017; 26: 818-821.
18. Laurant M, van der Biezen M, Wijers N, Kontopantelis E, van Vught AJAH. Nurses as Substitutes for Doctors in Primary Care. Cochrane Database of Systematic Reviews 2018; 7: CD001271.
19. Graham-Clarke E, Rushton A, Noblet T, Marriott J. Barriers and Facilitators to Non-medical Prescribing—A Systematic Review and Thematic Synthesis. PLoS One 2018; 13: e0196471.
20. Richards J. Addressing the Crisis in Access to Primary Care: A Targeted Approach. CD Howe Institute, 19th September 2024. (www.cdhowe.org).
21. Lee S, Mahl S, Rowe B. The Induced Productivity Decline Hypothesis.: More Physicians, Higher Compensation, Fewer Services. Health Care Policy 2021; 17(2): 90–104.
22. Pym H. Many Pharmacists to Vote on Cuts to NHS Services BBC, 19th September 2024 https://www.bbc.co.uk/news/articles/c1e8755xv01o.
23. NHS England Atlas of Shared Learning. Cuckoo Lane Surgery: An Innovative Nurse Led General Practice Delivering High Quality Care. 29th August, 2018 (https://www.england.nhs.uk/atlas_case_study/cuckoo-lane-surgery-an-innovative-nurse-led-general-practice-delivering-high-quality-care/).

24. Lenzen S and Birch S. From Population Numbers to Populations Needs: Incorporating Epidemiological Change into Health Service Planning in Australia. Social Science & Medicine 2023; 328: 115972.
25. Ono T, Lafortune G, Schoenstein M. Health Workforce Planning in OECD Countries: A Review of 26 Projection Models from 18 Countries. Organisation for Economic Cooperation & Development, Paris, 2018.
26. NHS Scotland. An Integrated Health and Social Care Workforce Plan for Scotland. 2019.

CHAPTER 6

# Economics and Pandemics

**Abstract** It would seem remiss, in such a volume, not to reflect on the role of economics during the recent Covid-19 pandemic. It went wrong for health economics, given its lack of visibility at a time when the management of scarcity—the lifeblood of economics—was key. But, likewise the management of resources during the pandemic was also a disaster for some countries and parts of the world. So, what could economics have contributed with respect to informing how we manage resources in the midst of the pandemic (allocations of resources to testing, ventilation and temporary hospital sites) and considerations of 'health versus the economy' more widely? Much policy deception lies in government consistently blaming current crises on the past pandemic, when the key to success was that of preparation. What is required, from an economic point of view, is a coordinated system (i.e. public) with high levels of spending; this combination seeming to have worked best with regard to pandemic outcomes. Also 'health versus the economy' can also be characterised as false dichotomy, or at least incomplete, in the sense that we can also think, within the same framework, of 'health for the economy'. These are two parts of the same framework, and which is invoked depends on where we are in terms of progression of any given pandemic. Internationally, too, vaccine provision, would be both fairer and more efficient if machinery for dealing with vaccine research, development and production and distribution were to follow principles of global common goods.

© The Author(s), under exclusive license to Springer Nature Switzerland AG 2025

C. Donaldson, *Financing Health and Social Care*,
https://doi.org/10.1007/978-3-031-86769-9_6

**Keywords** Value of life · Covid-19 · Collective action · Privatisation · Lockdown · Health vs economy · Vaccines · Global common good

*It may sound odd to say this, but, when planning this book, I considered not having a separate chapter on pandemics. Covid-19 policy-making was not good for health economics. On one hand, this is strange given that management of scarce resources—the lifeblood of (health) economics—was front and centre during the pandemic. But, (health) economics experts were absent at the podium and in expert advisory committees. To me, this was puzzling, and written about at the time* [1]. *But I was also encouraged to write this chapter on reading the excellent scientific memoir of a famous epidemiologist who was involved in providing much of the key advice during the pandemic who said 'We didn't hear enough from economists…'* [2].

Particularly in times of crisis, politicians do not wish to recognise limits by talking about management of scarce resources. However, during the Covid-19 pandemic, it is likely, too, there were unseen biases in favour of disciplines seen as more 'scientific'—like virology (obviously) and epidemiology. Perhaps economics was being conducted in the background alongside epidemiological modelling. But, generally, 'social science'—and I see the discipline of Economics as very much a *social* science—seemed relegated in its importance.

That is the end of my moan. Hopefully, the preceding chapters have demonstrated the important role of economics in post-pandemic recovery. This chapter simply seeks to round things off in addressing the role of economics in preparing for future pandemics, and, thus avoiding mistakes of the recent past. As it turns out, too, in writing the preceding chapters, the realisation came that much of what has been said can be applied to the Covid-19 (and future) pandemic(s). For example, what do ideas of demand-side socialism and the economics of collective action have to say about international comparisons of which systems (public or private) did better during the pandemic? Further, economics can also inform how we manage resources in the midst of the pandemic, addressing wider question such as 'health versus the economy' and narrower, but equally important ones, such as allocations of resources to testing, ventilation and temporary hospital sites. Finally, we turn to global health issues such as vaccine provision?

We will address these questions pretty much in that order, but, first, a caveat. Statements about which countries did better than others are tricky. Evidence continues to unfold and many national reviews are still ongoing. It is nevertheless important to recognise that people died in the most horrific circumstances, often alone, health and social care workers undertook their occupations in the most challenging situations and long-Covid cases are growing [3]. Hence, along with being just a health economist and not an expert on infectious diseases, my initial hesitancy in producing a separate chapter. But, to help us focus, we can draw lessons from earlier chapters, along the lines of the questions listed above. Perhaps, misdirections of politicians can be averted if some of these 'lessons' are taken on board.

## Who Did 'Best'?

To establish a baseline, I am going to resort to the ultimate outcome, mortality, and to the work of the *Covid-19 Excess Mortality Collaborators* published in *The Lancet* in April of 2022 [4]. This work provides an assessment of excess mortality—that is, mortality rates over and above what would normally be expected for all causes, including Covid-19, during the period 1 January 2020 to 31 December 2021 compared with data from up to 11 years previously—across 191 countries and territories.

From Table 6.1 it can be seen that, globally, the rate of deaths per 100,000 population of 39.2 meant that there were 5.95 million deaths attributed to Covid-19 over the two-year period. However, the number of excess deaths was nearly 3.07 times that; reaching 18.2 million. There is no question that countries such as South Korea, Australia and New Zealand performed exceptionally well with low levels of reported Covid-related deaths and even lower (in two cases, negative) excess death rates. Next would come the Nordic countries, especially Norway, where, again, excess death rates are less than those for Covid-19. Interestingly, Sweden, with its more laissez-faire approach of 'living with the virus' [2], did worse than its near-neighbours on Covid-related deaths but no worse than Denmark on excess deaths, and it still performed better than the UK on both counts. All of the UK's larger European neighbours performed better on Covid-related deaths, but not necessarily so on excess mortality. Recognised as the first major European country to experience the initial wave, it is not surprising that Italy is the worst performing on excess mortality, although the UK is worse than Italy with

**Table 6.1** Excess mortality during the Covid-19 pandemic (2020–2021) and 2022 health expenditures per capita

| *Country* | *Reported Covid-19 mortality rate per 100,000* | *Estimated excess mortality rate per 100,000* | *Health expenditure per capita (from Table 2.1), $PPP* |
|---|---|---|---|
| Global | 39.2 | 120.3 | |
| Australia | 4.7 | −37.6 | 5445 |
| New Zealand | 0.5 | −9.3 | 4812 |
| South Korea | 5.4 | 4.4 | 4224 |
| Denmark | 29.6 | 94.1 | 5052 |
| Finland | 16.1 | 80.8 | 4645 |
| Norway | 12.8 | 7.2 | 6239 |
| Sweden | 77.2 | 91.2 | 5310 |
| France | 97.4 | 124.2 | 5248 |
| Germany | 66.4 | 120.5 | 6448 |
| Italy | 120.6 | 227.4 | 3324 |
| Spain | 114.1 | 186.7 | 3633 |
| Canada | 41.9 | 60.5 | 5331 |
| USA | 130.6 | 179.3 | 10,331 |
| United Kingdom | 130.1 | 126.8 | 4552 |

respect to Covid-related deaths. Finally, Canada and the USA provide an interesting contrast to each other as well as with the UK; with Canada performing better than the other two on both outcome measures, the US and UK performing equally (badly) in terms of Covid deaths and the US performing worse in terms of excess deaths.

Lots of factors will be determining such rates, and especially differences between them; things like pre-existing levels of health inequality, the age distribution of the population, treatment of care home residents and even things like geographical proximity of members of the population to each other. But what might economics tell us? We will attempt to address this question by reference to some of the countries listed.

## The Key Combination: Collective Action, Integration and Health Spending

As the UK lurched through lockdowns and other Covid-19 restrictions over 2020–2021, there seemed to be little progress in addressing the pandemic. Inevitably, we kept returning to the basic public health interventions—encouraging handwashing, physical distancing and mask-wearing—which, through an interesting combination of collectively motivated individualistic actions, saved lives. Then came successes of new treatments for Covid-19 and the vaccination programme which further pointed to a key element for success: the need for collective action. New treatments were evaluated in robust trials only through the collective efforts of physicians, researchers, research funders, the NHS, and research participants. Vaccinations, too, were developed with extensive public funding and best delivered within the collective framework of the NHS. Having initially thought that the area of pandemics would be the most difficult in terms of finding support from Bevan in *In Place of Fear*, it turned out to be one of the easiest, as the following illustrates. In discussing how advanced societies tend to opt for collective solutions (e.g. pure water supplies, food standards) to many of their challenges, he states:

> The same is true in relation to contagious diseases. These are kept at bay by the constant war society is waging in the form of collective action by men and women who are paid fixed salaries. Neither payment by results nor the profit motive are relevant. (p. 99)

The UK's test-and-trace programme provides an interesting juxtaposition to further illustrate the point. Expertise already existed in collectively funded settings of the NHS and environmental health departments in local authorities. This works well because testing and tracing rely very much on local knowledge and the ability to integrate with other local services. Establishing private contracts at a national level to employ providers without such expertise, and who are disconnected from local services and communities, was nothing short of disastrous. Furthermore, the ideal test-and-trace system should actually be quite small. This is for twin reasons of health maximisation and efficiency. Where test-and-trace is established as a true preventive measure (note countries like South Korea and Australia), it involves identifying only small numbers of initial cases and tracing their contacts so as to avoid a pandemic in the first place. Such effectiveness, combined with being small, means resources are used efficiently and the opportunity costs from lives lost and diversion of health resources from non-Covid-related activity is minimised. In the UK, we built a test-and-trace system that was constantly chasing the virus, as opposed to stamping it out, partly because it was too late to do the latter by the time our system was established.

These challenges reflect, for me, the most neglected part of the post-pandemic debate; we, in the UK, were simply not prepared. Better-prepared countries have two main characteristics. First, as can be seen from the final column in Table 6.1, they tend to be high spenders on publicly funded health systems. This gives them the ability to spend more on public health; Eurostat data showing that Germany is particular good example of this [5]. Such systems, such as the Nordic countries and Korea, thus have the capacity to fight pandemics on multiple, integrated, fronts. Successive UK governments have been responsible for the erosion of total healthcare spending and, in particular, expenditure on public health, with administrations over the past 14 years being more culpable. Not only that, but in policy dealings regarding the pandemic, the UK Government seemed to want, as far as possible, to privatise the virus response. This could, of course, be based on genuine belief, but is not evidence based.

The second, related, characteristic is that of integration and coordination. This is best illustrated by the call by Governor Cuomo of New York on 31 March 2020 for all parts of the US healthcare system to come together to address the pandemic. Despite being the world's highest spender on healthcare, the system lacks the potential for integration, and thus collective action, that comes with public funding. Private insurance, focused on the care of individuals when they become ill, does not cope well with major public health threats.

## Market Failure: Managing the Virus Response

In addition to market failure offering a justification for the publicly funded systems and approaches to managing scarcity referred to throughout the book, there are several ways in which this notion could have been extended to help manage policy reactions to the pandemic once it was upon us. Some of these may have been happening. If so, apologies to policy-makers and health economics colleagues who were aiding them.

### *Harnessing Market Failure*

Overall, market failure, as a concept, could have been better harnessed with respect to policy-making. Remember, market failure arises when markets struggle to account fully for important characteristics of commodities; rendering their allocation sub-optimal relative to when governments intervene. During the pandemic, the commodities which received much attention were within events, hospitality and tourism sectors and the ability of participation in such activities to spread the virus. The argument would be that, if we allow such sectors to open up unchecked (or with limited attempts to manage distancing and mask-wearing), threats to health would not be accounted for in subsequent market transactions.

An alternative is to recognise market failure and use it as a framework helping us see a way forward. There are two key components to this. First, in a market with no Covid-related regulations, we know that there would be a whole set of transactions into which consumers and providers would be happy to enter. However, due to the existence of the virus, such transactions are either limited or prohibited. From experience prior to and during the pandemic, it should be possible, sector by sector, to make reasonable estimates as to the economic damage caused by the market failure induced by pandemic-associated regulations. But this is not enough. Second, a forecast is required as to whether, within time, the levels of economic activity experienced prior to the pandemic would be returned to or, at least, to what extent. In short, if such estimates can be made, along with a reasonable forecast as to the future trajectory of the sector, this would give a reasonable assessment as to the amount of subsidy required to maintain a sector whilst continuing to address the pandemic.

### *Who Shall Live? Fuchs Revisited as the Covid-19 Tide Approached*

In 1974, a classic book, *Who Shall Live?*, was published by Basic Books [6]. Its author was Stanford University Professor, Victor Fuchs, and the book is symbolic of the birth of health economics. The post-war era of continued growth in public services was coming to an end, combined, ironically, with growing abilities to treat patients and increasing public expectations of what our health care systems might deliver. Thus, all over the world, governments and their health care systems were now coming to terms with how to allocate limited resources across the claims of various patient groups and, in the case of public health, the wider population at large. Old examples were of rationing access to dialysis for older renal patients. But, even more recently, England's National Institute for Health & Care Excellence (NICE) has had to contend with deliberating on access to costly drugs to provide short extensions of survival for people in the final stage of life due to their cancer; some of which have been refused for provision via the NHS.

Such controversies over 'who shall live?' inevitably entered into prevention and care settings of the NHS as we addressed the ongoing Covid-19 crisis. The more immediate 'who shall live?' issues were around access to tests and ventilation. Amidst all the talk of 'ramping up' and the drive to mass testing, priorities were not clear. Although not made explicit to the public, multi-layered cost-benefit calculations were likely going on in the policy background. But who was being prioritised? It seemed that we were focused on producing and doing as much tests as possible, when, and especially when we plainly did not have enough capacity to come close to testing every NHS staff never mind population member, it would have seemed to make sense to focus on key workers and also the most vulnerable.

Further, once capacity began to get up to speed, the 'test-test-test' mantra proposed by the World Health Organisation was unclear as to its purpose. So-called mass testing would further divert nursing and laboratory resources from other much-needed care activities. Also, a claimed mass-tester, such as South Korea, was actually conducting very few tests in the early stages of the pandemic. This was because their testing was done in early stages of disease emergence and combined with isolation and rigorous contact tracing which never seemed to become feasible in the UK. In blunt terms, by the time it was feasible to do it in the UK, the mass screening ship had sailed, the best use of additional test capacity being in disease surveillance, so enabling better decision-making along the disease pathway.

More drastic 'who shall live?' dilemmas arose as we moved towards considerations of access to ventilation. Clinicians faced decisions on whether a young person with a decent chance of survival should take precedence over an older person who is severely ill and unlikely to live anyway. For those, health economics is better hovering in the background providing general principles to support the experts upon whom we ultimately rely—the clinicians. We cannot deny that we placed those experts in really tough situations with regard to deciding 'Who shall live'? A key part of this, which was not (explicitly) addressed during the pandemic, was the related question of 'what is the value of life?'

### *Valuing Human Life in the Time of Covid-19*

Early in the pandemic, it was often claimed that the value of lives saved from responding to the pandemic had been inflated relative to the usual value of a prevented fatality (VPF) used in public policy-making and, thus, relative to lives saved in other health and social programmes.

The usual VPF for use in UK public policy is around £2 m. As a society, we place implicit limits on the value of human life through decisions to limit resource allocations to the NHS and its various treatment and prevention programmes. The VPF was created to aid such decisions. But the fatalities prevented are probabilistic. For example, if 100,000 people were each asked to state their maximum willingness to pay for a 1/100,000 reduction in the risk of death over the coming year, and each gave a value of £20, a VPF of £2 m (£20 × 100,000) would emerge from aggregating the values across the 100,000 asked. What is actually valued is a (small) risk reduction. It is from posing more-sophisticated survey questions of this nature to representative samples of the general public that the VPF is derived. The 'mean' VPF is then applied to all cases of lives saved, regardless of demographic characteristics; so some element of equity is actually built into how it is used.

That claim of an inflated VPF was based on estimates of lives saved by lockdown relative to what otherwise might have happened, and combining this with costs arising from reduced gross domestic product and other harms also resulting from lockdown [7–9]. At a VPF of $2 m, the break-even length of lockdown was estimated to be 5–6 weeks. Such analyses are important given that, in other circles, lockdown, and its length, were being discussed [2]. To inform this (and other) debate(s), are there reasons why the VPF might have been higher, and, thus, a justification for rapid and even ongoing survey research to re-estimate it? There are four main reasons as to why this might be the case.

First, the magnitude of risk reductions upon which the VPF is built is different than for Covid-related risks, the latter being substantially higher on average, although varying across age groups [10]. When mortality risk changes are large, the VPF is likely to underestimate the social benefits arising from risk reductions [9]. This concern dissipates, however, if moving into a world comprising less-serious variants of the virus.

Second, it has been demonstrated that the public place premiums on certain types of ('dread') risks. This has been shown in the case of accidents involving group death (e.g. rail) or being trapped (such as in fires either at home or in a public place), even when the baseline risk for such events is often smaller than for a road fatality (on which the VPF is based) [11]. Such elements of dread, such as less-familiar and poorly understood risk, potential for isolation from family and friends, and even a lonely death, existed during the pandemic.

Third, much dread arises because we are dealing with a highly infectious virus. In surveys, the value attached to risk reductions tend not to account for such 'externalities'. Some (admittedly, unspecified) premium would be required to be added to the VPF to account for the fact that not only do we care about, but actually have a vested health interest in, ensuring risk reductions for others [12].

Finally, where groups are identifiable, there is a further tendency to inflate the VPF. Sometimes this is referred to as the 'rule of rescue' [13]. Where groups are vulnerable, as in the case of those in BAME groups and older people in care homes during the pandemic, the values may be inflated even further. Ironically, the social care debacle demonstrated that, contrary to these arguments, policy was deflating, rather than inflating, the value of such lives. Some may argue that, if we were to value life *years* as opposed to lives, then a reduced VPF for older people is appropriate. Although this argument is consistent with many valuation studies of the sort used to derive the VPF, one is reminded here of the US Environmental Protection Agency's dropping of a 'seniors discount' on the VPF in the early 2000s due to adverse reactions received in a series of public hearings on the matter [14]. Policy then seemed to flip by giving priority for vaccine access to those in older age groups.

All of the above could have been addressed via more-extensive empirical survey research of the sort used initially to derive the VPF [15]. Of course, it is important to point out that, the above is not an argument for a permanent step-change in the VPF. An inflated value may have been justified pre-vaccines. But, as the virus now moves to being endemic and we are in a state of pandemic recovery, a more-regular VPF could now be utilised in evaluating pandemic preparation versus other competing health policies and interventions.

## Bringing It All Together: An Economic Framework for Managing Health vs the Economy

During the pandemic, we seemed to be managing issues separately when they could also have been dealt with within a wider framework, recognising the trade-offs that were inevitably taking place. In this section, such a framework is outlined, based on the principles of marginal analysis outlined in Chapter 4 and on a paper I published with my colleague Craig Mitton in August 2020 [16]. We used the example of investing in activities to manage population health versus the opening of the economy from lockdown. Although lockdown was controversial [2], the principle expounded could be applied to many other sets of trade-offs at the time and in manging post-pandemic recovery now. We will focus, here, on controlling R. Do you remember 'R', the reproduction rate for the virus? This is also controversial, because there is more to controlling pandemic than R [2]. But we used it by way of illustration.

Of course, beyond a particular level of R (and background prevalence and incidence), the economy and health considerations go hand-in-hand. That is, at certain levels of disease, R must be controlled. But economics still has a lot to offer as a way of thinking and, thus, in contributing to honest debate about emerging trade-offs once R is curtailed. Once we had done our best to control R, new questions began to emerge which then required considerations of managing health and the economy together, as opposed to the prior stage (often due to lack of preparation) whereby health took precedence.

### *Marginal Analysis and Emergence from Lockdowns*

Recall from Chapter 4 that marginal analysis refers to the fact that assessment of costs and benefits is best addressed 'at the margin'. The focus is on the benefit gained from the next unit of resources, or that lost from having one unit less. In choosing between health care programmes, the question is not one of whether to resource one whole programme and none of the other. Rather, it is one of balance between the two. This simple way of thinking could have been used in earlier stages of the pandemic and even in preparation for it.

Often, the thought process behind marginal analysis is better described via a sequence of conceptual diagrams—see Fig. 6.1. The assumptions, to illustrate, are that we are now in a zone where the background level of infection is still significant but in which R is less than 1. We are, of course, aware that R differs by subgroups, across time and by location, but this does not deflect from the substance of the argument that trade-offs with the economy, whether at local, regional or national levels, can be made; and, indeed, were being made. The ‘benefits’ being traded off refer to some abstract notion of aggregate community well-being. Such benefits can arise from individual and private sector activity, but, in the current context, is heavily overlain and intertwined with public ‘bads’ and negative externalities (in the form of communicable disease), and, conversely, with improvements delivered by public goods and positive externalities (e.g. future protection). Therefore, given that only collective (i.e. not individual) actions can deliver such public goods and internalise such externalities, the framework is one proposed for use and adaption by government and other public agencies.

For purposes of illustration, let us say that such community benefit can be monetised and so presented on the same scale (or axis) as costs (Fig. 6.1a). Diagrams to the left of each of the eight parts in Fig. 6.1 illustrate marginal costs and benefits of reducing R from 1 to 0 whilst those to the right illustrate the same for opening the economy. In the latter, we include all sectors; public, private and civil society.

First, we invoke the necessary notion of diminishing marginal benefit, whereby the marginal benefits of reducing the R-value from 1 is positive but gradually reduces. Let us say that in the range of R = 0.7–1.0, marginal benefit reduces only very gradually (1b), after which, due to it being less critical, a sudden drop off in MB occurs before it continues on a more-regular downward slope (1c). Accordingly, and to be clear, as we reduce R, the total benefits are greater and greater, but the increases, in terms of the marginal social value of the corresponding health gains, are less and less. Hence, the downward sloping marginal benefit (MB) line for R and, correspondingly, for ‘Opening the economy’ (1c and 1d). Of course, we would recognise that, in the latter case, people may debate which sectors, or even which parts of sectors, are more or less valuable, even at the margin. However, even within sectors, we assume that the most-needed parts will be opened first, or, of course, never close. To aid presentation, assume the marginal costs (MC) of reducing R or economic expansion are constant and equal (1e). The question then becomes, given, on any particular day, a particular starting point for each of R and the economy, where do we go from here (1f). From 1g, it can be seen that the gap between MB and MC (or the MB/MC ratio) at the chosen starting point for the economy is greater than at the starting point for

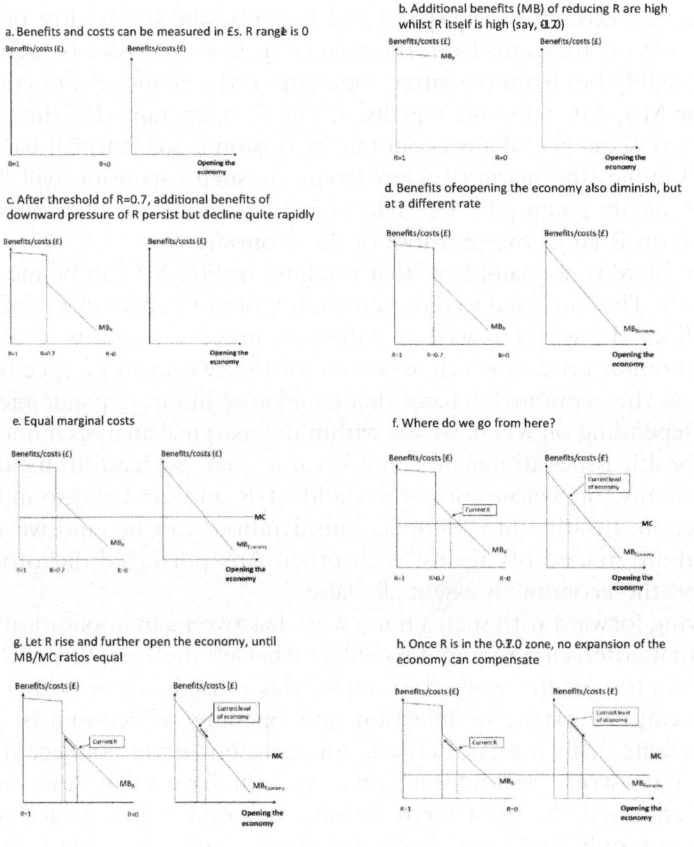


**Fig. 6.1** Great big marginal analysis: the theory. **a** Benefits and costs can be measured in £s. R range is 0–1. **b** Additional benefits (MB) of reducing R are high whilst R itself is high (say, 0.7–1.0). **c** After threshold of R = 0.7, additional benefits of downward pressure of R persist but decline quite rapidly. **d** Benefits of reopening the economy also diminish, but at a different rate. **e** Equal marginal costs. **f** Where do we go from here? **g** Let R rise and further open the economy, until MB/MC ratios equal. **h** Once R is in the 0.7–1.0 zone, no expansion of the economy can compensate

R. Thus, the economy can expand and R can be allowed to drift upwards as we trade-off the gains from the former against the losses (which there will inevitably be) from the latter. Opening of the economy can continue until the MB/MC ratios are equalised. The final diagram (1h) shows that, when a consequence of any economic expansion is for R to fall back into 0.7–1.0 range, the marginal gains from any such expansion will be too small to justify going past a certain point, beyond which the gains from focusing on R far outweigh those of the economy.

Note there is no claim here that the lines in Fig. 6.1 can be measured accurately. They are used to represent an important debate that took place throughout the world as well as a thought process to aid its resolution. It is a thought process which accounts for the two main perspectives on 'health-vs-the-economy' debates that could arise in future pandemic planning. Depending on where we are within the marginal analysis framework, either health issues dominate, only because they go hand-in-hand with the economy, or, below some threshold of R and/or background level of infection, health and economic considerations can be, and we would contend are, traded off against each other. Any portrayed dichotomy of health-vs-the-economy is essentially false.

Moving forward with such a framework has two main implications. The first is that criteria are required to reflect what we mean by 'benefit' [17]. In the context of the worked example, this must be done with respect to reducing R, extent of infection and opening of economies. Many governments defined sets of criteria for each, but never connected them in one framework. Second, and relatedly, nor have many governments openly admitted the need for trade-offs, not only within which loss of life may not only occur but also be tolerated. Indeed, it might be argued that deliberately not recognising trade-offs then allows avoidance of such uncomfortable truths. Even when below some critical threshold (like 0.7 in our example), a small increase in R will result in more infections and, as just alluded to, risk to life.

Such issues require debate and evidence on at least two key things: the critical range within which concern for R and background infection levels take over any concern even for incremental opening of the economy, a range which may, of course, vary across jurisdictions and more explicit use of values of health and life which already exist and are used in public policy [18, 19]. Their use, ultimately, means facing up to the question of the value to be placed on life and health versus opening the economy at the margin, accepting that that value may change according to whether we are above or below a critical value of R.

### *Relating the Framework to Common Pandemic Scenarios*

At the time of writing our initial article, all talk was of the R-value. At that time, even an R of 0.7 was seen as critical, largely due to the accompanying background levels of the virus. Above this level, a full lockdown may have been considered. Then we entered a world of partial lockdowns, which may even be the furthest governments can venture politically should a new virus come along with no accompanying vaccine. Also, questions faced by politicians and officials at their briefing sessions became more and more nuanced and sophisticated as time progressed. In this sub-section, we illustrate how the above framework can be adopted and used to help with thinking through, and even justifying, policy stances taken. The key theoretical driver in any case is the notion of diminishing marginal (social) benefit.

As can be seen in Fig. 6.2, and with full lockdowns less likely to be tolerated by the public, it is possible to adapt the framework for partial lockdowns. A full lockdown may be represented by column A in Fig. 6.2, whilst a more partial one may be represented by column B. Multiple thresholds, encompassing 'wack-a-mole' and 'circuit breakers', could even be accommodated by more-sophisticated versions of the framework.

At the briefing sessions of many leaders and officials, questions are frequently asked which allude to new laws and guidelines with respect to developing pandemic policies being inconsistent. On 10 September 2020, Nicola Sturgeon, then First Minister of Scotland, reported that her niece had quizzed her on why she could see her friends in school but not outside of that setting. The First Minster claimed 'To be fair, that's not an unreasonable question'. True; but the answer lies in thinking 'at the

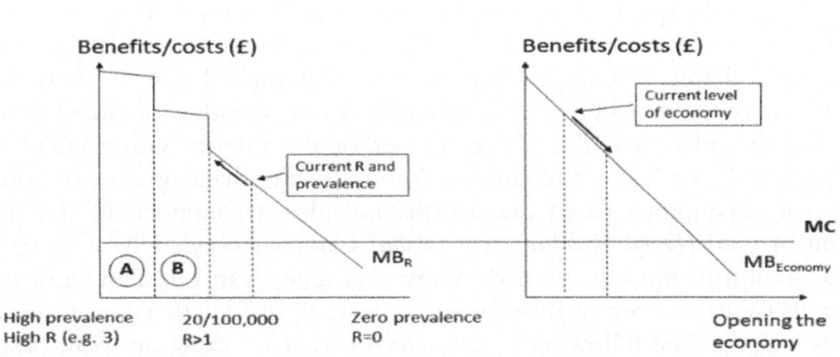


**Fig. 6.2** Multiple thresholds and partial lockdowns

margin' as espoused in our framework. Quite simply, the marginal social benefit of going to school is greater than meeting one's same friends in a more-social setting. The former is worth it in terms of social benefit, whilst, at that moment, the latter was not. Technically, and due to the notion of diminishing marginal benefit, it lies further down (or along) the $MB_{Economy}$ curve in Fig. 6.2. The same applies to situations of 'schools vs hospitality' when coming to decide on which might be subject to greater restrictions in the case of more-general spread of the virus. Having said that, public reaction to delayed opening of the hair and beauty sector in some countries perhaps indicated that the marginal (social) benefit is greater than was initially perceived by decision-makers.

Access to care homes has been hugely controversial. Strong cases were being made to ensure that such visitations can take place for the sake of the well-being of care home residents. Application of 'thinking at the margin' here might have allowed for safe entry (i.e. with PPE) of one designated visitor, given that the marginal gain from this is likely to be significantly higher than for each additional visitor. Even so, it is likely that such visitation permits would increase risks of cases of Covid arising in such settings. This may require a more precise use of the framework along the lines of considerations of the value of life, which could even be supported by empirical analysis of the trade-offs that carers, potential visitors and care home residents are willing to take on.

## The Vaccine

Back in 2020, over 3000 people (including 115 international personalities and 19 Nobel Laureates) issued a joint appeal to global leaders, international organisations, pharmaceutical companies and governments to adopt legal measures ensuring the availability of Covid-19 vaccines for all and free of charge [20]. Around that time, I was at an online meeting of the social business community, led by the ideas of Nobel Peace Laureate and (currently) Chief Adviser of the interim Government of Bangladesh, Professor Muhammad Yunus. Yunus challenged us to come up with economics-based calculations and ideas to support the declaration of *COVID-19 Vaccines as a Global Common Good*. I have to say I was doubtful. But encouraged by my colleague, Jean-Luc Perron of the Yunus Centre for Social Business in Paris, we worked with Yunus to make this happen. The following is summary of what we came up with, based on the work of Economics Nobel Laureate Elisabeth Ostrom [21, 22].

Of course, the need for this was illustrated by the behaviour of governments of advanced economies at the time, negotiating with vaccine developers to establish advance-purchase arrangements. For example, the UK Government signed a deal for access to a further 90 million vaccines on top of the 100 million doses of the Oxford University vaccine developed with Astra Zeneca. This, along with claims about the need to recover research and development costs and meet the demands of shareholders was driving up prices, which, without an alternative arrangement for funding and provision, would exclude many (likely the majority) of global citizens from access to the vaccine(s), to the health, social and economic detriment of us all.

### *The Vaccine as a Global Common Good*

Scientific consensus at the time was that, ultimately, the only way, definitively, to eradicate the pandemic was to have a vaccine administered to all inhabitants of the planet. However, this was not being recognised in policy actions. A 'tragedy of the commons' was emerging whereby selfish behaviour leads to adverse communal outcomes. Indeed, the some 25% of the world's population remaining unvaccinated would bear this out.

Globally, people had acted to eradicate Covid-19 within countries, through actions such as handwashing, distancing and wearing of masks and other personal protective equipment. We did these things for others as well as ourselves, and without which our abilities to undertake all actions—economic, social, self-interested or unselfish—would have been even more seriously impaired. Our point was that the same applies internationally. With viruses knowing no geographic boundaries, we have to act to help each other. Otherwise, we may never be able to return to the extent of previous cross-border collaborations for economic and social progress. Avoiding a tragedy of the commons on an international scale would require equitable access to vaccines for all people, irrespective of age as well as gender, ethnicity, country and other social and economic factors; thus rendering vaccines a global common good.

### *What Would Be Required?*

Rapid development no doubt led to great costs, which, as indicated above require a return on any private investments. Nevertheless, much of these investments came from the public purse. It should be recognised, too, that a vaccine represents a common good for the pharmaceutical industry, as it will permit them to practice in a world unencumbered by Covid-19. For these combined reasons, information issued by the private sector, scientists, and authorities, needs to be timely, accurate, clear, complete, and transparent. The research results should be in the public domain, making the vaccine available to any production facility that pledges to operate under strict international regulatory supervision and only to such facilities.

There are pre-existing models, too, which would allow this to happen. Three key pillars would be required to operationalise *Covid-19 Vaccines as a Global Common Good*. First, would be a set of ***clear principles and commitments*** of the sort articulated in Box 6.1.

**Box 6.1 Principles for Creating Covid-19 Vaccines as a Global Common Good**

- vaccines approved by regulatory authorities to be treated as 'essential generic medicines'.
- patents to be placed in the public domain against cost-based compensation for laboratories.
- the production and distribution of vaccines to be accessible to all countries, without priority nor exclusivity, and thus regarded as a 'global common good'.
- allocation rules and pricing policies to be transparent, under the watch and reporting of an arbitrator whose decisions are final.

Organisations such as the World Health Organisation (WHO) are well placed to broker agreements on such principles. The second pillar is an ***operator***, a not-for-profit organisation with capacity to mobilise contributions as well as interface across the international community, the health systems of the different countries for implementing mass vaccination, and the pharmaceutical industry for manufacturing vaccines at a given price. The Global Alliance for Vaccination and Immunization (GAVI) presents a ready-made model. GAVI was created 20 years ago to accelerate vaccination against childhood diseases in developing countries.

The third pillar is an ***industrial force***. The pharmaceutical industry is needed for mass producing the vaccines hoped for. The prospect of abandoning the exploitation of patents in favour of a global common good, available in open source, and of obtaining compensation at cost for the investments made for the development of these vaccines, to the exclusion of a net profit, may seem unattractive. But, as articulated above, there are wider financial benefits at stake for industry in combination with the goodwill from contributing to global healthy longevity.

Around that time, I even conducted a simple cost-benefit calculation for a vaccination programme for the UK, which, by extension, also applies to vaccinating the rest of the world—for free! This is outlined in Box 6.2.

**Box 6.2 Costs and Benefits of Vaccination Programme in the UK, January–June 2021**

Vaccines have prevented 46,300 hospital admissions up to end of June 2021 [1].

Assume each admission would have a cost of £1000 per day with a length of stay of 15 days. So, total cost of hospitalisations averted = £15,000 × 46,300 = £694.5 m.

If the cost of an AstraZeneca jab is estimated at £3 [2]. NHS England data show that around 70 m jabs had been administered over the same time period, at a total cost of £210 m. Government 'upfront costs' for manufacturing and development of vaccines have been estimated at around £900 m [3].

Net resource cost of the vaccination programme, therefore, is around **£415.5 m**.

Over same period, according to NHS England, 14,000 lives were saved. Assuming a value of a prevented fatality of £2 m, the total value of lives saved = **£28b**.

So excluding the value of non-fatal illness averted and other knock-on impacts on the economy, the net value of the vaccination programme to the UK is around **£27.6b.**

Over the coming months, as hospitalisations continue to be averted, there would likely be net savings in resource costs. Although compelling for one rich country, the UK has met a considerable part of development costs which would not be required for generic production. By extension, therefore, a strong case exists for vaccinating the world.

1. https://www.gov.uk/government/news/covid-19-vaccine-surveillance-report-published
2. https://www.google.ca/amp/s/www.statista.com/chart/amp/23658/reported-cost-per-dose-of-covid-19-vaccines/
3. https://www.bmj.com/content/372/bmj.n421

## Conclusions

The Covid-19 pandemic illustrated that populism can be bad for your health. Note the performance, in terms of Covid-related deaths, in countries—such as Brazil, the UK and the US—run by populist leaders whilst in the midst of the pandemic. These were leaders who could not resist the temptations to go-late and leave-early from more restrictive and collective public health policies aimed at controlling the spread of the virus and, ultimately, saving lives. Their governments, too, showed no prior commitments to public funding of their health care systems to a level of capacity whereby major threats to public health could be better coped with. Blame and associated misdirection is placed on the pandemic itself, when in these terms, we simply were not prepared. Post-pandemic, this should remain a concern for many voters.

Economic frameworks exist to help both prepare for pandemics and also manage them. Better economic analysis would have allowed those under pressure 'at the podium' to justify different levels of lockdown strategy, articulate that apparent inconsistencies are not so after all, to consider if (and why) some initial decisions on economic expansion are better reversed and to weigh up difficult balances, such as that of care home access. The basic messages would be that (1) these policy directions can be supported by a framework backed by economic theory and which has been regularly applied in international health and social care contexts worldwide and (2) in many cases, the straightforward answer as to why some actions were allowed whilst others not is simply on the basis of (marginal) social benefit of each. Trade-offs are inevitable, but not recognised in policy. If they had been, then as well as well as better analysis and public debate, overall human welfare could have been better optimised.

Finally, politicians of many advanced economies also seemed to take great pride in their accumulation of vast stocks of vaccines ignoring the fact that funds required to mobilise around *COVID-19 Vaccines as a Global Common Good* pale into insignificance relative to what will be required to address ongoing economic recession consequent on non-eradication. But despite this financial case, such mobilisation requires attention to break-throughs in economic thinking beyond the conventional ways of thinking about the economy and of doing business. Can we really live, once again, with newspaper headlines about the richest countries being served with vaccines first and about staggering profits for pharmaceutical companies and laboratories and stock prices for their shareholders whilst most of the world's population is left behind? Even our self-interest is better served by an alternative.

## References

1. Donaldson C and Mitton C. Donaldson C and Mitton C. Coronavirus: Where Has All the Health Economics Gone? International Journal of Health Policy and Management 2020 (https://www.ijhpm.com/article_3835_0a34bcb000efe565636d6df38e0980c8.pdf).
2. Woolhouse M. The Year the World Went Mad: A Scientific Memoir. Sandstone Press, Muir of Ord, Scotland, 2022.
3. Davis HE, McCorkell L, Moore Vogel J, Topol EJ. Long Covid: Major Findings, Mechanisms and Recommendations. Nature Reviews Microbiology 2023; 21: 133–146 (https://doi.org/10.1038/s41579-022-00846-2).
4. Covid-19 Excess Mortality Collaborators. Estimating Excess Mortality Due to the Covid-19 Pandemic: A Systematic Analysis of Covid-19-Related Mortality, 2020–21. Lancet 2022; 399: 1513–1536.
5. Eurostat Statistics Explained. Preventive Health Care Expenditure Statistics, March 2024. (https://ec.europa.eu/eurostat/statistics-explained/index.php?title=Preventive_health_care_expenditure_statistics#:~:text=Germany%20spent%20%E2%82%AC30.0%20billion,Italy%20(%E2%82%AC11.4%20billion).
6. Fuchs VR. Who Shall Live? Health Economics and Social Choice. Basic Books, New York, 1974.
7. Miles D, Stedman M and Heald A. Living with COVID-19: Balancing Costs Against Benefits in the Face of the Virus. National Institute Economic Review 2020 https://doi.org/10.1017/nie.2020.30.
8. Rowthrom R and Maciejowski J. A Cost-Benefit Analysis of the COVID-19 Disease. Oxford Review of Economic Policy 2020; 36(S1): 38–55.
9. Colmer J. What Is the Meaning of (Statistical) Life? Benefit-Cost Analysis in the Time of COVID-19. Oxford REVIEW of Economic Policy 2020; 36(S1): 56–63.
10. Spiegelhalter D. Use of 'Normal Risk' to Improve Understanding of Dangers of COVID-19. BMJ 2020; 370: m3259.
11. Chilton S, Jones-Lee MW, Kiraly F, Metcalf H, Pang W. Dread Risks. Journal of Risk and Uncertainty 2006; 33: 165–182.
12. Jones-Lee MW. Altruism and the Value of Other People's Safety. Journal of Risk and Uncertainty 1991; 4: 213–219.
13. Hadorn DC Setting Health Care Priorities in Oregon: Cost-Effectiveness Meets the Rule of Rescue. JAMA 1991; 265: 2218–2225.

14. Seelye KQ and Tierney J. EPA Drops Age-Based Cost Studies. New York Times 8th May 2003.
15. Jones-Lee MW. The Value of Changes in the Probability of Death or Injury. Journal of Political Economy 1974; 82(4): 835–949.
16. Donaldson C and Mitton C. Health Economics and Emergence from COVID-19 Lockdown: The Great Big Marginal Analysis? Health Economics, Policy and Law 2022; 17: 227-231 https://doi.org/10.1017/S1744133120000304.
17. Peacock S, Richardson J, Carter R, Edwards D. Priority Setting in Health Care Using Multi-attribute Utility Theory and Programme Budgeting and Marginal Analysis (PBMA). Social Science & Medicine 2007; 64(4): 897–910.
18. Chilton S, Nielsen JS, Wildman J. Beyond COVID-19: How the Dismal Science can Prepare Us for the Future. Health Economics 2020; 29(8): 851–853.
19. Lancsar E, Swait J, Mitton C, Breunig R, Mirk M, Huynh E, Donaldson C. Preparing for Future Pandemics: A Multi-national Comparison of Health and Economic Trade-Offs. Health Economics 2023; 1–19. https://doi.org/10.1002/hec.4673.
20. Link to website. See Lancet paper.
21. Yunus M, Donaldson C, Perron J-L. COVID-19 Vaccines for the Global Common Good. Lancet Healthy Longevity 2020: 1(1); https://doi.org/10.1016/S2666-7568(20)30003-9.
22. Ostrom E. Governing the Commons: The Evolution of Institutions for Collective Action. Cambridge University Press, Cambridge 1990.

CHAPTER 7

# Conclusion: The Price of Demand-Side Socialism in Health and Social Care

**Abstract** This concluding chapter begins with a question; that of whether the reader likes what they see, currently, in terms of a disintegration of collectively funded health care systems. If the answer is 'no' but that there is nothing to be done, the forecast is one of the emergence of multi-tier systems whereby those able and willing to pay receive better and quicker care. This may go even further in the sense of such groups articulating a case for tax breaks to help fund their march into the private sector. Encouraged by several vested interests, that case might even be made (naively and erroneously) on the basis of helping out the NHS. In fact, it would constitute robbing the NHS of staff who could otherwise have been publicly funded and used to treat people according to their needs. The latter is the alternative prescription; a collectively funded system designed to overcome the excesses and unfairness of market failure and even extending this into social care. This applies globally, too. We need to encourage accelerated implementation of Universal Health Coverage. Coming back to the UK and other advanced economies, a reset is required whereby the tax consequences of what is proposed are explained to and supported by the public. What may seem like a cost is actually an investment in avoiding greater costs and unfairness in the future; an investment *In Place of Fear 2.0*.

**Keywords** Taxation · Universal Health Coverage · Pay

© The Author(s), under exclusive license to Springer Nature Switzerland AG 2025

C. Donaldson, *Financing Health and Social Care*,
https://doi.org/10.1007/978-3-031-86769-9_7

Hopefully, I have convinced you that there is an economic basis to Aneurin Bevan's initial vision for an NHS 'In Place of Fear' and that the way forward for health and social care, in the UK and elsewhere, is some form of demand-side socialism. I say 'some form' because each country will have a different starting point and, therefore, have to think of different policies for getting there.

There are many reasons for current dissatisfaction with health care systems, which then make arguments for moving away from demand-side socialism more compelling. We are already seeing wealthier people voting with their feet into privately financed care. This is dangerous because although most countries have learned the advantages of some sort of collective insurance, which in the UK and other countries means financing via taxation, this is now under threat of sever erosion. Despite no countries' health systems being the same, the commonalities are greater than the differences. The key is that of public financing. In thinking about whether to move away from this, then we need to ask ourselves two questions: can things go on as they are? Do you like the alternatives that might be proposed?

## Crossing the Tipping Point: Do You Like What You See?

I think, for most people, the answer to the first question is 'no'. If we do not do something, we will keep returning to issues such as long waiting times, people thinking more and more about turning to private payment for treatment, and subsequent threats to health and income. More and more, it would seem that the average person in the population is feeling and seeing the very real cracks in our systems.

Regarding the second question, what is most likely to happen? It would be easy to now make some attempt at scaremongering and say that the alternative is a US-based system with all the high costs that would impose on individuals and businesses in the financing of insurance premiums and the inequities that would arise in terms of access to care. This path is unlikely, however, as we are all still locked into a single system of taxation.

But there could quite conceivably be a more-realistic tipping point of another nature. With more and more people electing for privately-funded care, due to long NHS waiting times, it may not be long before the vocal middle class are asking for tax breaks to help pay for this. (We may think this is unlikely, as it does not happen in other areas, such as education, where there is an even greater use of privately funded provision. However, in this sector, subsidies have been achieved, but, most obviously, on the supply side, through exemptions for Value Added Tax. Although this subsidy may soon disappear, there are routes to demand-side subsidies, too, through things like gifts, trusts, offshore bonds, all of which can be created or taken out in ways that are tax-exempt.)

Returning to health and social care, it is conceivable to see the claim being made that private insurance is helping the NHS by relieving pressure on it. This is an illusion. In fact, this move would amount to a subsidy for privately financed care that would be robbing the public sector of valuable doctor and nursing time that could be used to treat people on waiting lists, who, due to being less wealthy, are likely to be in greater need. Indeed, the list might even grow, and delays in treatment might cost more. It may not be a case of 'hello USA!', but we would still end up with a system costlier and less equitable than we have now. A slightly more tepid anti-change rallying cry might, therefore, be 'hello Australia!' with its complex mix of public and private finance and provision and associated tax subsidies.

Australia were 'late to the party' in terms of publicly funded and comprehensive health care, and their mixed system reflects this starting point. By the 1980s, when they finally got there, a strong private insurance industry existed and had to be accommodated in any reforms. By getting in early, in the 1940s, the UK and many other countries did not have to deal with making compromises with the insurance industry. This is a great advantage going forward that we should think hard about before throwing it away. As well as the higher costs and great inequity involved, as we can see from Australia's experience, there would be no going back. If you do not like the look of this, then, logically, there can be no alternative than to support the current system, but there is a *quid pro quo*.

## The Prescription

Before we get to that *quid pro quo*, in terms of lessons from the rest of the book, the first would be to focus any discussion of 'privatisation' on the above; ensuring no breakdown in the public financing of care. With respect to provision, the issues are different. Each system has many different categories of provider and the key is to ensure that they work according to the principles and objectives of a publicly funded system.

These systems also need to incorporate social care not only in place of fear but because care in homes and care at home are becoming more and more populated by people with genuine health needs. The arguments for public funding for such groups, based on aspects of market failure, apply to such populations as much as for those covered by health care systems. Indeed, a strong case for a fully integrated system of health and social care exists rather than thinking about, at least in the UK context, a National Care Service that would be separate to an NHS; that would threaten any advances in integrated care that have already occurred.

Whatever local entities exist or are created in the future, they need to come to terms with recognising and managing scarcity of resources. The principles for doing this need to be more embedded in the system and the best way to achieve this is through education. The curricula of management education need to be, in my view, rebalanced away from management fads that are often taught in MBA programmes towards those disciplines that would aid the efficient and equitable management of scarcity; those of ethics and research methods aimed at enhancing the evidence base, and including health economics. Likewise, the curricula for general practitioners and medical specialists as well as other health professions, many of whom go on to manage our health care systems and the large amounts of, nevertheless scarce, resources that involves.

Much of the above applies to pandemic preparation. The key combination, from an economic perspective is collective action with the public health capacity that comes from being a relatively big spender on health care in general. The latter can be mitigated somewhat by test-and-trace preparation, of the sort that we, in the UK, do not seem to be investing in right now. Other methods we could invest in are frameworks that balance health against other aspects of life and accounting for situations in which the value of life used in public policy might change. Work on some of that could have gone on during the pandemic and, for future preparation, could start now. Finally, we need international frameworks and agreements for cost-effective and fair vaccine provision in situations of future existential threats.

## Universal Health Coverage

Occasionally, I have referred to specific countries other than the UK and also stated that the arguments presented apply more widely. The movement around the globe towards Universal Health Coverage (UHC) reflects that relevance. However, on attending a major international health economics conference in Africa in the summer of 2023, I was struck by the lack of progress in several countries towards UHC. Being the host nation for the conference, South Africa was, naturally, a case which received a lot of attention.

I write this as a non-expert in health care financing in lower-income countries and with apologies to those making strenuous efforts with respect to implementing UHC. No doubt, any lack of progress towards UHC is exacerbated by fiscal challenges across the globe. However, I was left thinking whether we, as health economists, are somewhat complicit. The impression I came away with was that there seems to be a view that health systems in more-advanced economies have things right and that UHC cannot be declared in particular jurisdictions until that is the case there too.

Many arguments centred around ensuring legal entitlement to pre-defined health benefit packages. This is great for providing work for academic lawyers and health economists, but, to me, means that health economics is getting in the way of UHC and giving politicians excuses for not following through on the promise. This may seem contradictory to some readers, so what do I mean?

To me, the notion of legal entitlement to specific benefit packages is doomed to fail. No advanced economy has such entitlements available to them. We have rights to be *considered* for just about any treatment. Even when access is agreed, we may have to wait. Given levels of affordability in lower-income countries the packages to which one would have legal entitlements to would have to be very restrictive. The idea of a health benefit package, too, poses major questions of feasibility and ignores basic principles of opportunity costs and the margin. Components of a package cannot be discretely defined; not all patients benefit to the same extent, some will be included in terms of public coverage when they should be excluded, and some excluded when they should be included. Defining, or even regularly updating, such a package becomes an impossibility. Whenever attempts to do this have been embarked upon in more-advanced economy settings, we end up with a set of principles to guide decision-making but not an actual defined package. In the background to this, too, significant variations in provision persist in the systems of more-advanced economies which often go unrecognised in such debates. We, in more-advanced economy settings, recognise such imperfections but continuously work to review and repair them as we go along. If we seek to start with such repairs in place we will never start.

In terms of paying for the system, there will be compromises in order to bring everyone on board. For example, Table 2.1 shows that, despite claims in more-advanced economies as to having single-payer systems, this is not the case. Although in a minority, elements of private payment exist across all countries. Again, we need to accept this as part of the starting point.

My solution would be for countries to declare that they are enacting UHC. Give access to primary care for all, but have that as a gatekeeper to the rest of the system. Have everyone contribute, but allow private insurance on top. Allow physicians to practice in the private part of the system, but restrict the amount of time they can devote to this. Finally, principles and legal entitlements do not get rid of scarcity of resources; so, put in place the education and structures that allow national and local level priority setting in health resource allocation to be managed fairly.

We are deluding ourselves that the health systems of more-advanced economies are somehow perfect, and, whilst continuing, in lower-income countries, to disallow access to care for those most in need, are in danger of allowing such (false) perfection to be the enemy of the merely very good in continuing the establishment of UHC. Perhaps my own suggestions are deluded, but they should at least be costed out in different environments in order to assess the 'art of the possible' instead of assessing costs and cost-effectiveness of different care packages that may never be implemented.

## New 'Contracts' with Professions and, Especially, the Public

If you have managed to get this far, there are two questions you might have wanted or expected me to answer given that I am an economist and the questions relate to money—how much to pay doctors and how much to spend on the health and social care systems as a whole. At least, I suspect, you will have that expectation if based in the UK. The questions may or may not pertain further afield, but the clone-like nature of economic policy across the globe means they may indeed be relevant in other countries. Another caveat is that I cannot answer these questions, at least not precisely.

To explain, the first question is what should doctors and others be paid. In many countries there are review bodies for that. They know more than I and, in the UK, are required to take account of several factors such as retention, variations in local and regional labour markets, NHS and overall economic strategy (especially inflation) and principles of equal pay for equal work [1]. For what my own view-as that is all it would be—is worth, I believe we should pay people enough to ensure our best students go into health (and social) care, stop staff haemorrhaging to expensive agencies only to be reemployed at more expensive rates or to working overseas, and recognise the heroes of Covid beyond clapping on our doorsteps. I am sure at least some of that is accounted for in the criteria listed, but, beyond that, I couldn't possibly comment! One thing we can say for certain, due to comprehensive analysis over several decades, is that, up to 2010, doctors and nurses were well paid relative to both inflation and other workers in the UK economy, but since then this has declined [2].

The second question takes us right back to the beginning of the book and is that of how much to spend. The general consensus, at least for the UK and including my own view, is MORE! But, answers to this will be personal. It also depends on what question we want to answer. If we want to address the question of where the best pay-offs are in terms of health gains at the margin, then pumping more resources into the NHS is not necessarily the answer. There are two other rivals for investment here; the communities in which people live and social care. The former (through things like housing and other health-promoting facilities) might do better at generating health gains. Likewise, social care has a dual role to play in aiding early discharge from hospitals and in preventing people entering hospitals in the first place. Time and again, politicians will respond to NHS crises by spending more on the NHS. It seems obvious and, of course, plays to the electorate, when better health-promoting solutions might be to spend our taxes elsewhere. This is why the LSE-Lancet Commission on the Future of the NHS recommended percentage increases in social care spending on par with what they recommended for the NHS [3], and, I suspect, to some degree, is likely to apply to other countries.

Another major question is that of sustainability. This is not all coming from me, as three major reviews undertaken in the UK in the last five years, one which I was a member [3] have all recommended funding increases [3–5]. The most recent was that of Lord Darzi [3] which focused more on infrastructure and the capital investment gap that now exists in the NHS, but did also state that funding increases need to be restored to historical levels, which amount to 3–4% annually in real terms [5]. This is supported by the other two reviews, those of the LSE-Lancet and the BMJ Commission on the Future of the NHS [3, 5]. In addition to capital spending, recommendations to restore this annual level of spending increase take account of: future population pressures, specifically the need to manage more chronic and mental health conditions and do this in community settings; improvements in innovation (some of which will save resources and some of which will cost more). Recommended increases in social care spending are roughly equivalent to the calculations presented for Scotland in Chapter 3.

The tax consequences of such increases have been estimated by the LSE-Lancet Commission as equivalent to a 1p increase in each of basic, higher and additional income tax rates, employer and employee national insurance contributions and Value Added Tax VAT over a four-year period followed by higher increases in income taxes and NIC subsequently. However, these tax burdens could be distributed differently—for example, with higher increases for those in higher income brackets and even adding new higher income brackets to add even more progressivity. There are many other sources of taxation (e.g. on wealth or inheritance) that could be considered to ease the burden on those sources mentioned whilst still acting progressively. Stealth taxes, through not increasing threshold levels in line with inflation, can also effectively raise more money as can raising the national insurance rate paid by employers, but not workers, and eliminating the regressiveness of national insurance, whereby earnings above £50,000 per annum are 'taxed' at two per cent whilst the rate is eight per cent for earnings up to £50,000. As of 2024, the 3–4% increase in real spend recommended by the above Commissions seems to have been adhered to by the UK's new Labour Government, achieved largely through (some of) these other means and without resorting to increases in income tax. However, Commission estimates were made before large percentage pay increases were (rightly, in my view) also agreed by Labour. These will take up much of the 3–4% in a way not accounted for by the Commissions. Likewise, proposed increases in VAT impacting on general practice and many social care providers, which give the impression of giving with one hand and taking with the other. However, the reason VAT applies is because they are private entities (see Chapter 3). Exemptions would be possible. However, the situation, especially in the case of social care, shows the mess that politicians have now created with respect to social care and the need for some kind of model of demand-side socialism to sort it out. Indeed, things like a VAT exemption might even be used as some of carrot for provide providers to play ball with a publicly-funded system.

Thus a 'contract' with the UK population is required which will likely require other tax increases. Also, we should not discount borrowing. Even in the US, prominent Modern Monetary Theorists [6] have promoted this notion:

> As long as federal government commits to making the payments, it can always afford to support these programs. What matters is our economy's long-run capacity to produce the real goods and services people will need. (p. 157)

This is contrary to the mantra of 'If you cannot afford it, you cannot have it' espoused to the UK House of Commons in July 2024 by newly elected Chancellor of the Exchequer, Rachel Reeves. In many respects, this quotation betrays the dilemma of the modern Left, both in the UK and elsewhere. Politicians now pander to the feeling amongst many relatively well-off voters that, somehow, they are poor and cannot afford, or do not wish, to pay more taxes. As Margaret Thatcher once put it, when addressing the Conservative Women's Conference in 1988:

> I can't help reflecting that it has taken a Government headed by a housewife with experience of running a family to balance the books for the first time in 20 years – with a little left over for a rainy day.

Thus, although it may seem that, even on the Left, we are all Thatcher's children now, there are sound economic theories which run counter to this well-known 'fallacy of composition' that we should run the economy like a household. As well as Modern Monetary Theory, other such theories derive from the ideas of Keynes and Polanyi [7, 8]. Indeed, one of Keynes' best-known phrases, in a BBC Radio address in 1942 was 'Anything we can do, we can afford'. Sensible borrowing, to support infrastructure and social programmes in particular is perfectly feasible in economic terms. A parallel is that of buying a house; many of us could never achieve this without borrowing the money in advance. At the time of borrowing, we cannot afford it, but we can have it!

If we jump back to Table 2.1, it shows that we can choose to do this. It has long been known that the main driver of health expenditure is national income [9], and the UK is a wealthy country. Probably next, in terms of driving spend, is technological change [5], often meaning that we can do more for those who we could not necessarily treat before—with new drugs and less-invasive surgery. Changing demographics, especially ageing, are often referred to as drivers, but there is little evidence of this [10, 11]. This can be observed in Table 2.1 where it can be seen, broadly, that richer countries spend more *per capita* on health care. Furthermore, if we look at countries such as Sweden, what this shows is that we can choose to spend more through the public purse.

To reiterate, if you do not like what you see then the key is not to throw away our basic system thinking that will resolve anything. It always amazes me that, in recent times, politicians and the media in general have not paid heed to the reviews I have mentioned. Having been commissioned by the current UK Government, perhaps they will pay heed to Darzi. 'Hard decisions', which keep being referred to, apply to all, and include those who can afford to pay more in taxation. Without striking such a contract with the public, all that I, as a health economist, can predict is that we will keep returning to these points of crisis, although it will gradually get worse as society continues its current trend towards greater inequality. That inequality, in the form of multi-tierism, will extend to health and social care and may even reach the tipping point to which I have referred and whereby government even ends up funding the breakdown of health and care systems via tax breaks. These tax breaks, through supporting increased private funding of care, will further rob the NHS of the precious doctor time it requires to treat those in greater need but without the tax breaks to fund any private insurance. The moral hazard engendered by that private insurance will ensure that we, as a society, will pay more and more relative to the bill from being locked in together, as we currently are. Greater cost, as well as more inequality, will ensue. We will still have an NHS, but an NHS in name only, borne of political double-speak of a parallel privately funded system 'helping the NHS' rather than genuine principals of efficiency, equity and caring for each other. If you do not wish to see your government actually sponsoring the break-up of our NHS, when the fairer way is for society to wake up and recognise that fairness and efficiency are best served by a system funded through progressive taxation, then you need to encourage them to strike that contract with you. The current UK Government is now part way towards that contract. But you need to hold them to the rest. In other countries, look to doing the same in moving towards or maintaining UHC. Some countries are more explicit than others about this commitment, and its benefits for economic efficiency as well as equity. Returning to my two main go-to countries for comparison with the UK, and despite some of my criticism of them, note, first, this statement from Health Canada in 2021 [12]:

> Canada's publicly funded health system reduces administrative costs compared to private systems, ensuring that funds are spent more efficiently, ultimately benefiting the economy, including businesses. By focusing on prevention and equitable access, public health care also reduces the long-term economic burden of disease, which can positively impact the overall business environment.

Secondly, in addressing the Royal Australian College of General Practitioners in October 2019, Australian Health Minister Greg Hunt, stated:

> The Medicare system is one of the most cost-efficient health care systems in the world.

Bevan would likely be encouraged. If you agree with the case made in this volume, then you might also support his contention, in 1952, that:

> ... no government that attempts to destroy the Health Service can hope to command the support of the British people. The great argument about priorities is joined and from it a free Health Service is bound to emerge triumphant. (*In Place of Fear*, p. 116)

Many UK politicians have since issued similar statements of support. But, often, here in the UK and elsewhere, and as we have seen throughout this volume, there is a yawning gap between the rhetoric and the reality. Hopefully, you are persuaded that the economics of Bevan's contention adds up and needs to be brought front and centre into health and social care policy, helping to reduce that gap and (re)create the case for demand-side socialism in health and social care; *In Place of Fear 2.0.*

## References


1. NHS Pay Review Body. Thirty Seventh Report 2024. Office of Manpower Economics, London, 2024.
2. Elliott R. The Economics of the UK Health and Social Care Labour Market: How Labour Economics Can Inform Policy Towards the Frontline Labour Force. Oxford University Press, Oxford, 2024.
3. Charlesworth A, Anderson M, Donaldson C, Johnson P, Knapp M, McGuire A, McKee M, Mossialios E, Smith P, Street A, Woods M. The Future of the NHS: What Is the Right Level of Spending Needed for Health and Care in the UK? The Lancet 2021; 397: 2012–2022 (https://doi.org/10.1016/S0140-6736(21)00230-0).
4. Lord Darzi. Independent Investigation of the NHS in England. OGL, Crown Copyright, September 2024.
5. Appleby J, Leng G, Marshall M. The BMJ Commission on the Future of the NHS: NHS Funding for a Secure Future. British Medical Journal 2024; 384e079341.
6. Kelton S. The Deficit Myth: Modern Monetary Theory and How to Build a Better Economy. John Murray, London, 2021.
7. Keynes JM. The General Theory of Employment, Interest and Money. Macmillan, London 1936 (reprinted 2007).
8. Polanyi K. The Great Transformation. Farrar & Rinehart, New York, 1944.
9. Parkin D, McGuire A and Yule B. Aggregate Health Care Expenditures and National Income: Is Health Care a Luxury Good? Journal of Health Economics 1987; 6(2): 109–127.
10. Barer M, Evans RG, Hertzman C and Lomas J. Ageing and Health Care Utilization: New Evidence on Old Fallacies. Social Science and Medicine 1987; 24(10): 851–862.
11. Kallesstrup-Lamb M, Marin AOK, Menon S, Sogaard J. Ageing Populations and Expenditures on Health. The Journal of Economics and Ageing 2024; 29: 100518.
12. Government of Canada. Report on the Economic Impact of Health Care. Health Canada, 2021.

# Index



© The Author(s), under exclusive license to Springer Nature Switzerland AG 2025

C. Donaldson, *Financing Health and Social Care*,
https://doi.org/10.1007/978-3-031-86769-9

**V**



**W**

The manufacturer's authorised representative in the EU is Springer
Nature Customer Service Centre GmbH, Europaplatz 3, 69115 Heidelberg,
Germany. If you have any concerns regarding our products, please
contact ProductSafety@springernature.com

Printed and bound by CPI Group (UK) Ltd, Croydon, CR0 4YY
30/09/2026
02225514-0005